This book is based on my need to learn to use encouragement as a tool to help you to develop your thoughts about what and how encouragement can be used as fuel to your success.

I0479137

SUCCESS THROUGH ENCOURAGEMENT

TABLE OF CONTENTS

- The benefits of using encouragement in the workplace
- The impact of encouragement on employee motivation and productivity
- The relationship between encouragement and employee engagement
- The role of encouragement in setting and achieving goals
- The importance of constructive feedback in encouraging success
- The impact of encouragement on team dynamics and collaboration
- Encouraging success through effective communication
- The role of encouragement in promoting a growth mindset

Chapter 2.

- The impact of encouragement on stress and mental well-being
- Encouraging success through mentorship and coaching
- The relationship between encouragement and creativity
- The benefits of encouraging a sense of ownership and accountability
- The role of encouragement in fostering a culture of innovation
- The impact of encouragement on employee retention and loyalty
- Encouraging success through recognition and rewards
- The importance of encouraging a balance between work and personal life
- The role of encouragement in developing leadership skills
- The impact of encouragement on overall organizational success

Chapter 3.

- The role of encouragement in overcoming obstacles and challenges
- Encouraging success through building resilience and perseverance

- The impact of encouragement on personal and professional development
- The relationship between encouragement and emotional intelligence
- The role of encouragement in fostering a positive and supportive work environment
- Encouraging success through active listening and empathy
- The importance of encouraging open communication and transparency
- The impact of encouragement on problem-solving and decision-making
- The role of encouragement in fostering a culture of continuous learning and improvement
- How can encouragement help you succeed
- What are 10 words that bring you inspiration
- What is the value of encouragement
- Why is encouragement important in life

Chapter 4.

- What is success through encouragement
- Understanding the power of encouragement
- Encouragement in the workplace
- Encouragement for personal growth
- Encouragement in relationships
- Encouragement for children and youth
- Encouragement in sports
- Encouragement in education
- Encouragement for those facing challenges
- The importance of self-encouragement
- Encouragement and motivation
- Encouragement in leadership
- Encouragement and team building
- Encouragement and positive reinforcement
- Encouragement and goal setting
- Encouragement and accountability

- Encouragement and perseverance
- Encourage others to succeed

Chapter 5

- Encouragement and resilience
- Encouragement and self-confidence
- Encouragement and emotional well-being
- Encouragement and stress management
- Encouragement and positive attitude
- Encouragement and time management
- Encouragement and communication skills
- Encouragement and problem-solving
- Encouragement and creativity
- Encouragement and innovation
- Encouragement and learning

Chapter 6

- Encouragement and personal development
- Encouragement and professional development
- Encouragement and change management
- Encouragement and conflict resolution
- Encouragement and decision making
- Encouragement and teamwork
- Encouragement and productivity
- Encouragement and effective delegation
- Encouragement and mentorship
- Encouragement and networking
- Encouragement and continuous improvement
- Encouragement and overall success.

Chapter 7

- Success Encouragement at home
- How can you encourage yourself
- What are examples of encouraging words
- What is the best motivation for success
- What is a good sentence for encouragement
- What are 5 synonyms for encouragement
- What are the 7 types of motivation

- What is a daily encouragement
- Why is encouragement important in school
- What are 2 words for encourage
- Why is encouragement important for a child

Chapter 8

- How can we encourage others in their hard times
- How do you respond to encouragement
- What is the meaning of encouragingly
- What does it mean to encourage someone
- Is encouragement the same as support
- What is something that encourages a person to do something
- How does encouragement improve performance
- Is encouragement an attitude
- What happens when you encourage
- How do you use encouraged
- What are the components of encouragement

Chapter 9

- What is an example of encouragement........
- What is encouragement motivation
- Who is your greatest source of encouragement
- Why encouragement is important in learning and development
- What encouragement does God give us
- What is personal encouragement
- How do you write a note of encouragement
- Overcoming Obstacles through Encouragement
- How do you stay encouraged by God
- What are the two ways of encouragement

Chapter 10

- What are the 3 main factors which can lead to success of a person?
- How Encouragement is the Key to Success
- What are the keys of success?
- What are the steps to success?
- 15 Steps to Achieving Success through Encouragement
- The Transformative Impact of Encouragement (from self doubt to self-assurance)

Chapter 11

CONCLUSION

<u>INTRODUCTION</u>

Success Through Encouragement is a strong idea that may assist people and groups in reaching their greatest potential. Consider a world in which all members of your team are encouraged to take chances, try new things, and learn from their failures without fear of failure. A world in which hard effort and commitment are rewarded, and trust and collaboration are the norm. This is the universe of Encouragement for Success.

It is a world in which clear and attainable goals are established, and the necessary resources and support are made available to assure success. It's a world where people and teams are encouraged to grow and reach new heights, and where continual improvement is encouraged.

Success through Encouragement is more than a catchphrase; it is a way of life. It is all about establishing a good and supportive atmosphere in which people may grow and attain their greatest potential. So why not embrace it and see how far you can get?

By embracing Accomplishment through Encouragement, you will unlock the power of optimism and support in yourself and your team, allowing you to do the seemingly impossible and fly to new heights of success.

CHAPTER 1

*Definition of Encouragement and Its importance in Achieving success

Encouragement is one of the key factors that make your business successful. It can be anything from a note of appreciation in a mailbox or a simple hug from a loved one, to coaching and helping other staff members improve their skills.

Encouragement is an essential factor in all human relationships. It is the positive response or reaction of people to others' actions or efforts. Encouragement is also a universal need, as every person wants to be valued and appreciated by his/her near and dear ones. When people feel that they matter in someone else's life, they are motivated to put their best efforts into making the relationship work better.

Encouragement is a powerful tool for achieving success. It serves as the catalyst for growth and development. A supportive environment is essential to success. Encouragement increases one's receptivity to feedback, opportunity and criticism, which are key components in identifying strengths and weaknesses in order to set goals, make improvements and achieve success.

Success through encouragement is the key to achieving success. Encouragement that leads to success depends on the one who does it and on whom it is done. It's a blessing for those who give because receiving encouragement can be a turning point in your life, but it's also a blessing for those being encouraged,

Success is not measured by how much money you make; it's measured by your progress and achievements. Never let our environment, people, or circumstances determine if we can succeed. It is our confidence, belief, and having faith in ourselves that will empower us to rise above any adversity and achieve greatness.

In life, there are two types of people: those who see obstacles as opportunities for success, and those who see obstacles as reasons to quit. Those who succeed get through difficult situations by taking whatever lessons they can from each one and using them to achieve greater success in the future. Those who fail often do so because they do not want to see the hard work that is required to make things happen, or they get discouraged when things don't go as planned — rather than adapting and coming up with a new plan. Successful people know what they have to do, as well as how much work it will take to get them there.

_____ *The Role of Positive Reinforcement in Encouraging Success

Positive reinforcement is the most effective and powerful tool for encouraging success because it encourages others to improve their behaviour, behaviour that you want them to repeat. The role of positive reinforcement in encouraging success is due to the fact that it helps direct people's attention to those aspects of their environment which have a high probability of success, thus differentiating from negative reinforcement which encourages continued behaviour by reducing the likelihood that an individual will be punished for it

Success achieved through encouragement is not due to the size of the accolades given, but rather the quality of reinforcement that inspires you to strive for improvement.

In today's fast-paced world, there is rarely room for error. Competitive hiring makes it even more important that you take time to engage with your candidates in a way that would make them feel successful. Encouraging a feeling of success through positive reinforcement can be an effective step toward encouraging success.

*The Benefits of Using Encouragement in the Workplace

Encouragement in the workplace is similar to a secret ingredient in a successful dish. It may enhance employee motivation and engagement by adding flavor, depth, and richness to the workplace culture. Consider a workplace in which every person feels like a member of a team, where their contributions are acknowledged and recognized, and where employees are enabled to fulfil their greatest potential. This is the type of environment that encouragement fosters.

Employees will feel more driven to undertake difficult assignments and will be more inclined to move outside of their comfort zones to attempt new things if they are encouraged. They'll be more interested in their work and more inclined to take ownership of their responsibilities, resulting in higher productivity and job satisfaction.

Encouragement has a significant influence on morale. It has the potential to foster a good and supportive work atmosphere in which people feel heard, understood, and valued. This may lead to improved relationships between managers and employees, as well as a more pleasant and cohesive team culture.

Encouragement may also act as a spark for creativity. Employees are more inclined to think outside the box and come up with inventive solutions to challenges when they feel secure in their talents and encouraged in their efforts. This can result in breakthroughs and a stronger competitive advantage for the organization.

Furthermore, encouragement can boost employee performance and lead to improved corporate results. It can also aid in the retention of top talent since employees who feel valued and appreciated are more inclined to stay with the organization.

Overall, encouragement is a strong weapon that may revolutionize the workplace and make it more interesting, productive, and pleasurable. It's a little investment with significant payoffs for both the corporation and its employees.

*The Impact of Encouragement on Employee Motivation and Productivity

When employees are unmotivated and unproductive, the organization lands in trouble. The impact of encouragement on employee motivation and productivity is one of the best ways to provide such a boost.

Having a positive attitude is one of the most important factors in an employee's success. A positive attitude influences every aspect of daily life, including how well they perform their job and how much they enjoy it. Encouragement is one of the best ways to start improving your employees' attitudes...

As the modern business environment becomes more dynamic and challenging, organizations are increasingly challenged to motivate their employees. Developing an effective leadership style is critical to developing productive teams that can maximize the potential of every individual in your organization. One of the most powerful and effective ways for leaders to influence employee behaviour is through effective encouragement. Individuals need encouragement from their leaders; employees are empowered by positive reinforcement, which generates greater performance and success for both individuals and teams.

Employees who feel supported and encouraged at work are generally happier, more engaged, and productive. They also enjoy a better quality of life. But it's possible to do too much or too little when it comes to offering feedback, which can be just as detrimental to people's self-confidence and momentum as criticism or indifference.

*The Relationship Between Encouragement and Employee Engagement

Success needs encouragement. The positive message and catchy phrase on this motivational poster inform employees that you care about them, their well-being, and their potential at work.

Employee engagement is a three-part cycle that begins with intrinsic drive. This can be accomplished through encouragement or the development of connections that foster positive behaviour and attitudes.

Encouragement can assist promote staff engagement and productivity. Employees who are encouraged by their bosses are more likely to be engaged, dedicated, and productive, according to three years of research. This means that firms who make an effort to encourage their employees profit from happy, loyal employees who surpass industry norms.

A number of studies, including those from Gallup and MetLife, have proven the link between encouragement and employee engagement. Employee engagement may be improved at all levels, including supervisors, peers, and individuals. Employee recognition is an excellent approach to foster a climate in which individuals feel free to pursue their dreams, address issues honestly, and offer credit where credit is due.

According to Gallup, a nice and supportive work atmosphere may increase employee engagement by 47%. This training will teach you how to utilize encouragement to foster supportive connections, boost team performance and productivity, and boost job happiness.

*The Role of Encouragement in Setting and Achieving goals

Encouragement is the act of encouraging people to strive towards their goals. Encouragement may be utilized to help achieve personal goals, but it also plays an important role in the business.

Encouragement is really important in attaining goals. According to research, encouragement can improve performance, self-concept, and competence, and good feedback is related with tenacity when confronted with difficult conditions. Encouragement is an excellent tool for supporting individuals in setting goals and then achieving them.

Encouragement is a critical component of success and is required for goal setting, achievement, and maintenance. Encouragement builds morale and confidence, propelling you to new heights. Without it, you may become bogged down in self-doubt and second-guess all of your efforts toward your objectives, undermining your drive. If you're seeking for some motivation to feed your inner motivator, keep in mind that encouragement does not always imply being too enthusiastic or cheerleading others; it should be a particular action taken in support of someone else's efforts.

To reach your objectives, you must be able to see a clear route forward. Reaching a goal when you don't know what it is or how to get there is tough, if not impossible.

Encouragement is more than a nice-to-have; it is required for goal-setting and success. It may help increase your confidence, relieve tension and worry, and keep you inspired to persevere during difficult circumstances. Without it, you may find it difficult to have the confidence and resolve to see your goals through to completion. So, don't be scared to seek for encouragement and assistance; it might be the difference between accomplishing and failing to achieve your goals.

*The Importance of Constructive Feedback in Encouraging Success

Constructive feedback is essential for promoting success. It reminds individuals of their strengths and inspires them to continue developing and learning. Successful individuals are those who can take criticism and utilize it to better their performance and abilities.

Constructive feedback is critical in fostering achievement, especially at the outset of your journey. Make sure to give clear and honest criticism on your performance so that it may be utilized to help you overcome any problems and develop.

Constructive feedback is important in promoting achievement since it gives you the confidence to perform better the following time.

Instead of attempting to make yourself appear nice when you hear constructive criticism, push yourself farther and strive harder.

Positive feedback is a great instrument for achieving achievement. A well-intended complement or encouraging comment may increase your confidence and assist you in reaching your objectives.

Success is a journey rather than a destination. The more successful you become, the more critical it is to continue to improve. Constructive feedback is essential in this process since it promotes achievement.

*The Impact of Encouragement on Team Dynamics and Collaboration

Encouragement has a very positive impact on team dynamics and collaboration. When individuals on a team feel encouraged, they are more likely to work together towards a common goal and express their ideas and opinions without fear of judgement or criticism. This kind of open communication and collaboration increases trust and allows for better understanding among team members. It also encourages risk taking and creative thinking, which can lead to innovative solutions to complex problems. Additionally, feeling encouraged can motivate team members to give their best effort and push them to perform at their highest level. Ultimately, by creating an atmosphere of support and affirmation, encouragement has the potential to improve team dynamics and collaboration significantly.

*Encouraging Success Through Effective Communication

Effective communication can play a key role in encouraging success. Open and honest communication that provides honest and constructive feedback and recognition can help create a sense of ownership and motivation in employees. Having open channels of communication where employees can ask questions, give feedback and get feedback can help employees understand the tasks at hand and how to be successful in meeting the organization's goals. Additionally, listening to employees' concerns and ideas can help an organization uncover new ideas and innovative solutions that can help it reach its goals more effectively. Encouraging success through effective communication also helps to create a culture of trust and understanding between management and employees, which can lead to a stronger, more productive workforce.

Encouraging success through effective communication can be achieved by expressing your confidence in the other person and setting a goal or a clear expectation. It is also important to show understanding and appreciation when the other person succeeds and providing constructive criticism if they fail. Effective communication is an essential part of developing relationships, setting and meeting expectations, motivating, and recognizing achievement. Communication should be tailored to the situation, the goal, and the individual in order to maximize success. Additionally, listening carefully and using verbal and non-verbal cues can help both parties to understand each other and foster trust and a collaborative spirit.

*The Role of Encouragement in Promoting a Growth Mindset

Encouragement can be an important part of promoting a growth mindset. It can be a powerful tool for motivating someone to reach their goals and instilling in them a belief that hard work and effort will result in positive outcomes. By recognizing successes, and celebrating accomplishments, a person can gain self-confidence and understand that their efforts to pay off. Positive reinforcement for taking risks and challenging oneself can be a powerful way to help a person understand that their effort can lead to growth. This helps create a strong sense of purpose and belief in oneself, which can drive progress and progress. Encouragement also builds relationships, strengthens communication, and helps to motivate someone to strive to reach their full potential. It allows someone to have an understanding that the ability to improve is possible. This is a cornerstone of having a growth mindset and is an important part of developing a successful and lasting growth mindset.

Encouragement plays an important role in promoting a growth mindset. It provides a sense of affirmation that enables individuals to believe in themselves and their abilities, which is essential to fostering a growth mindset. When people feel supported and encouraged, they are more likely to push past their limits, take risks, and have a sense of resilience when faced with challenges. Encouragement also reinforces positive thinking, leading individuals to become more optimistic about their ability to learn and grow. Finally, it promotes a culture of collaboration and respect in which everyone can participate and reach their full potential.

CHAPTER 2

*The Impact of Encouragement on Stress and Mental Well-being

Encouragement has a positive effect on stress and mental well-being. Encouragement is often described as an inner motivation, or inspiration that can help an individual gain confidence and maintain focus during stressful situations. Receiving encouragement and support can give someone the motivation and self-belief needed to confront their challenges, making them feel better equipped to handle stress. Encouragement is associated with greater emotional regulation, reduced anxiety and a decrease in depression and burnout. It is a valuable source of support, providing validation that helps boost morale and reduce feelings of stress and anxiety. It is also a key ingredient in building self-confidence, which in turn can contribute to overall mental health.

Encouragement also gives individuals a sense of control over their circumstances and increases motivation and a desire to keep striving. Finally, when people feel encouraged, they tend to take risks and take chances they wouldn't have taken otherwise. This allows individuals to find creative solutions to their problems, further reducing stress and enhancing well-being.

*Encouraging Success Through Mentorship and Coaching

Mentorship and coaching are both essential for helping people to achieve success in life. A mentor provides support, advice, guidance and knowledge that help an individual to identify their strengths, develop their skills and create achievable goals. A coach is focused on achieving a desired outcome, such as helping a person reach a certain level of proficiency or performance in a certain area. Coaches help their clients to stay on track, provide helpful feedback, and create plans of action that help to ensure that goals are met. When mentors and coaches work together, they provide an effective way of helping an individual to succeed in any field or endeavour.

Mentorship and coaching can be extremely beneficial when trying to encourage success in others. Through mentorship, a mentor can share their experiences, insights, and provide guidance on any challenges they face. Through coaching, a coach can provide tailored advice and feedback on the individual's development and help to ensure that the individual has a plan and steps to achieve success. By providing these tools, it can help to create a pathway for an individual to reach success, by building a solid foundation and support system for them to do so.

*The Relationship Between Encouragement and Creativity

Encouragement has been found to be a key factor in creativity. Research has found that encouragement of creative pursuits leads to improved creativity outcomes and a more positive attitude toward creative activities. This is due to the fact that encouragement provides individuals with greater confidence in their own abilities and allows them to explore and develop ideas in an open and trusting environment. When encouragement is combined with other forms of support, such as providing resources and facilitating connections, creativity is further enhanced. In addition, positive reinforcement and constructive feedback help to reinforce creativity. As such, encouragement has been identified as an important factor in stimulating creativity and fostering an environment that encourages creative growth and exploration.

Encouragement can have a positive impact on creativity. When a person is encouraged, they can be more motivated and inspired to think of new and innovative ideas. Additionally, they may be more willing to take risks and try out new things, both of which are important aspects of creativity. When people are encouraged and supported, they can also be more likely to explore their ideas and expand on them, leading to increased creativity. Ultimately, when people are given the right support and encouragement, they are likely to be more creative in their work.

Encouragement is a key factor in developing and cultivating creativity. Studies have found that people with supportive, encouraging environments often are more successful in finding innovative solutions to problems, which often involves a certain level of creativity. People with supportive and encouraging people around them also tend to be more comfortable taking risks, experimenting with new ideas, and thinking outside the box. This is because they feel safe and have the confidence to try out new concepts, knowing that someone is there to support and validate their ideas.

*The Benefits of Encouraging a Sense of Ownership and Accountability

1. **Increased Employee Motivation**: Encouraging a sense of ownership and accountability can give employees a greater sense of purpose, helping to improve motivation and job satisfaction.

2. **Improved Quality**: Employees who feel a sense of ownership in their work tend to be more meticulous and conscientious about the quality of their output.

3. **Increased Innovation**: Employees who are empowered to make decisions tend to be more innovative in their thinking.

4. **Greater Commitment to Projects:** Encouraging employees to take ownership of their work helps them to be more invested and committed to their tasks, leading to increased efficiency and productivity.

5. **Stronger Employee Relationships**: Establishing a sense of ownership and accountability promotes stronger relationships among employees, allowing them to work together to reach common goals.

*The Role of Encouragement in Fostering a Culture of Innovation

Encouragement plays a crucial role in fostering a culture of innovation.

Boosts morale: Encouragement can help boost the morale of individuals and teams, which in turn can lead to increased creativity and innovation.

Creates a supportive environment: A supportive environment where people feel encouraged to take risks and share their ideas can lead to a culture of innovation.

Promotes risk-taking: Encouragement can help individuals and teams feel comfortable taking risks, which is a key component of innovation.

Increases motivation: Encouragement can increase motivation and drive, which can lead to individuals and teams being more proactive in finding new and innovative solutions.

Fosters collaboration: Encouragement can help foster a sense of collaboration and teamwork, as individuals and teams feel supported in working together to find new and innovative solutions.

Supports experimentation: Encouragement can support experimentation and exploration, which are key components of a culture of innovation.

In conclusion, encouragement plays a vital role in fostering a culture of innovation by boosting morale, creating a supportive environment, promoting risk-taking, increasing motivation, fostering collaboration, and supporting experimentation.

*The Impact of Encouragement on Employee Retention and Loyalty

Encouragement can have a significant impact on employee retention and loyalty.

Improved job satisfaction: Encouragement can improve job satisfaction by making employees feel valued and appreciated. This, in turn, can lead to increased loyalty and a decreased likelihood of leaving the company.

Increased motivation: Encouragement can increase motivation and drive, which can lead to improved job performance and satisfaction.

Fosters a positive work environment: A positive work environment, where employees feel encouraged and supported, can lead to increased job satisfaction and a reduced likelihood of turnover.

Enhances relationships: Encouragement can enhance relationships between employees and their managers, leading to a stronger sense of trust and commitment.

Boosts confidence: Encouragement can boost the confidence of employees, making them feel more capable and capable of contributing to the success of the organization.

Recognition of achievements: Encouragement through recognition of achievements and contributions can lead to increased job satisfaction and a greater sense of purpose and fulfillment.

Overall, encouragement can have a positive impact on employee retention and loyalty by improving job satisfaction, increasing motivation, fostering a positive work environment, enhancing relationships, boosting confidence, and recognizing achievements.

*Encouraging Success Through Recognition and Rewards

Recognition and rewards can be effective tools for encouraging success.

Boosts motivation: Recognition and rewards can boost motivation by making employees feel appreciated and valued for their contributions and hard work.

Increases engagement: Recognition and rewards can increase employee engagement by making them feel more connected to the company and its goals.

Fosters a positive work environment: A positive work environment, where employees are recognized and rewarded for their achievements, can lead to increased job satisfaction and a reduced likelihood of turnover.

Enhances performance: Recognition and rewards can enhance performance by providing employees with a tangible reward for their hard work and achievements.

Promotes teamwork: Recognition and rewards can promote teamwork by encouraging employees to collaborate and support each other in achieving common goals.

Supports personal and professional growth: Recognition and rewards can support personal and professional growth by providing employees with a sense of accomplishment and a motivation to continue improving.

In conclusion, recognizing and rewarding employees can be a powerful way of encouraging success by boosting motivation, increasing engagement, fostering a positive work environment, enhancing performance, promoting teamwork, and supporting personal and professional growth.

*The Importance of Encouraging a Balance Between Work and Personal Life

Encouraging a balance between work and personal life is crucial for overall well-being and success.

Improves work-life balance: Encouraging a balance between work and personal life can help individuals maintain a healthy work-life balance, leading to improved physical and mental health.

Reduces stress: Allowing employees to prioritize their personal lives can reduce stress and burnout, leading to increased productivity and job satisfaction.

Enhances relationships: Encouraging a balance between work and personal life can help employees maintain and strengthen their personal relationships, leading to a more fulfilling life outside of work.

Increases motivation: Allowing employees to have a healthy work-life balance can increase motivation and drive, as they feel more energized and fulfilled in both their personal and professional lives.

Supports work-life integration: Encouraging a balance between work and personal life can help employees find ways to integrate their personal and professional lives, leading to a more fulfilling **and satisfying overall experience.**

Attracts top talent: Companies that prioritize work-life balance are more likely to attract top talent, as employees are increasingly seeking employers who support their overall well-being.

In conclusion, encouraging a balance between work and personal life is important for overall well-being, reducing stress, enhancing relationships, increasing motivation, supporting work-life integration, and attracting top talent.

*The Role of Encouragement in Developing Leadership Skills

Encouragement plays a crucial role in developing leadership skills.

Boosts confidence: Encouragement can boost the confidence of individuals, making them feel more capable and capable of taking on leadership roles.

Supports risk-taking: Encouragement can help individuals feel comfortable taking risks, which is a key component of leadership and innovation.

Fosters collaboration: Encouragement can help foster a sense of collaboration and teamwork, which are important skills for leaders to possess.

Increases motivation: Encouragement can increase motivation and drive, which can lead to individuals being more proactive in taking on leadership responsibilities.

Recognition of achievements: Encouragement through recognition of achievements and contributions can lead to increased motivation and a greater sense of purpose and fulfillment, which are important for developing leadership skills.

Promotes continuous learning: Encouragement can promote continuous learning and growth, as individuals feel motivated to seek out new opportunities for development and growth.

*The Impact of Encouragement on Overall Organizational Success

Encouragement can have a significant impact on overall organizational success.

Improves employee morale: Encouragement can improve employee morale, leading to increased job satisfaction and a reduced likelihood of turnover.

Boosts motivation and productivity: Encouragement can boost motivation and drive, leading to increased productivity and improved job performance.

Enhances collaboration: Encouragement can enhance collaboration and teamwork, leading to better decision-making and problem-solving.

Fosters innovation: Encouragement can foster a culture of innovation by promoting risk-taking and encouraging continuous learning and growth.

Attracts top talent: Companies that prioritize encouragement are more likely to attract top talent, as employees are seeking employers who support their growth and well-being.

Supports a positive workplace culture: Encouragement can support a positive workplace culture, where employees feel valued, supported, and engaged.

In conclusion, encouragement can have a positive impact on overall organizational success by improving employee morale, boosting motivation and productivity, enhancing collaboration, fostering innovation, attracting top talent, and supporting a positive workplace culture.

CHAPTER 3

*The Role of Encouragement in Overcoming Obstacles and Challenges

Encouragement plays a crucial role in overcoming obstacles and challenges.

Boosts confidence: Encouragement can boost confidence, enabling individuals to approach obstacles and challenges with a positive attitude and determination.

Promotes persistence: Encouragement can promote persistence and resilience, helping individuals overcome setbacks and keep moving forward.

Increases motivation: Encouragement can increase motivation, leading individuals to work harder and strive for success despite obstacles and challenges.

Provides support: Encouragement provides support, allowing individuals to feel like they are not alone in facing obstacles and challenges.

Recognizes achievements: Encouragement through recognition of achievements can provide individuals with a sense of accomplishment and a motivation to continue pushing through obstacles and challenges.

Fosters growth and learning: Encouragement can foster growth and learning by promoting continuous improvement and helping individuals develop new skills and strategies for overcoming obstacles and challenges.

In conclusion, encouragement plays a vital role in overcoming obstacles and challenges by boosting confidence, promoting persistence, increasing motivation, providing support, recognizing achievements, and fostering growth and learning.

*Encouraging Success Through Building Resilience and Perseverance

Encouraging success through building resilience and perseverance can lead to improved outcomes and overall success.

Supports perseverance: Encouragement can help individuals develop a strong sense of perseverance, enabling them to overcome challenges and achieve their goals.

Builds resilience: Encouragement can help individuals build resilience, allowing them to bounce back from setbacks and continue moving forward.

Promotes growth mindset: Encouragement can promote a growth mindset, where individuals view challenges and obstacles as opportunities for growth and learning.

Fosters problem-solving skills: Encouragement can help individuals develop problem-solving skills, enabling them to find creative solutions to challenges and overcome obstacles.

Increases motivation: Encouragement can increase motivation, leading individuals to work harder and strive for success, even in the face of adversity.

Supports continuous learning and improvement: Encouragement can support continuous learning and improvement, as individuals feel motivated to seek out new opportunities for growth and development.

In conclusion, encouraging success through building resilience and perseverance can lead to improved outcomes and overall success by supporting perseverance, building resilience, promoting a growth mindset, fostering problem-solving skills, increasing motivation, and supporting continuous learning and improvement.

*The Impact of Encouragement on Personal and Professional Development

Encouragement can have a significant impact on personal and professional development.

Boosts confidence: Encouragement can boost confidence, allowing individuals to take on new challenges and opportunities for growth.

Supports continuous learning: Encouragement can support continuous learning, as individuals feel motivated to seek out new opportunities for growth and development.

Increases motivation: Encouragement can increase motivation, leading individuals to work harder and strive for success in their personal and professional lives.

Promotes a growth mindset: Encouragement can promote a growth mindset, where individuals view challenges and obstacles as opportunities for growth and learning.

Enhances relationships: Encouragement can enhance relationships, as individuals feel supported and valued by those around them.

Recognizes achievements: Encouragement through recognition of achievements can provide individuals with a sense of accomplishment and fulfilment, promoting personal and professional growth.

In conclusion, encouragement can have a positive impact on personal and professional development by boosting confidence, supporting continuous learning, increasing motivation, promoting a growth mindset, enhancing relationships, and recognizing achievements.

*The Relationship Between Encouragement and Emotional Intelligence

The relationship between encouragement and emotional intelligence is that people with higher emotional intelligence are better able to receive and give positive reinforcement, and provide encouragement in order to boost their own and others' morale. It is a crucial tool for managing stress, achieving goals, and having meaningful relationships with others. With emotional intelligence, one can better understand and identify one's own and other people's emotions, and effectively respond to these in order to foster successful interactions. It is not enough to just be a good listener; those with higher emotional intelligence know how to act and react in a situation in order to promote positive interactions. This includes recognizing what encouragement is necessary, and providing it to others in a thoughtful, appropriate manner. Encouragement helps people build confidence, have courage, be hopeful, and ultimately succeed in whatever they are doing. This connection between emotional intelligence and encouragement demonstrates how important both are in cultivating healthy relationships, building resiliency, and providing meaningful experiences.

The relationship between encouragement and emotional intelligence is very positive. People with higher levels of emotional intelligence are more likely to provide encouragement to those around them. This can have a positive impact on those receiving the encouragement, as it can lead to greater self-esteem, motivation, and resilience. It can also help to strengthen relationships, as those receiving the encouragement will often respond in kind. Overall, it is important for people to recognize the value of providing encouragement to those around them, as it can have significant positive benefits.

The Role of Encouragement in Fostering a Positive and Supportive Work Environment

Encouragement is an important factor in fostering a positive and supportive work environment. Encouragement allows employees to feel that their efforts are valued and appreciated and gives them a sense of purpose in their work. It also helps to foster cooperation among employees and strengthens the team environment. Encouragement can also lead to increased motivation, productivity, and morale, leading to a more productive workplace. Finally, it can create an atmosphere of trust, where employees feel comfortable communicating openly with each other and are able to collaborate and cooperate to find the best solutions. All in all, encouragement plays a vital role in creating a positive and supportive work environment.

Encouragement is essential for fostering a positive and supportive work environment. It creates an atmosphere where employees feel motivated and appreciated, enabling them to work more effectively. It also helps boost morale, reduces stress and can create a sense of loyalty to the organization. Encouraging words or actions can be offered verbally, nonverbally or through rewards such as promotions or pay raises. Employees should be encouraged for successes, hard work and commitment to their jobs, as well as their creativity and willingness to take initiative. Additionally, fostering a supportive environment can help prevent burnout and conflict in the workplace. Ultimately, positive reinforcement can help make employees feel valued, leading to greater job satisfaction and productivity.

Encouragement plays a crucial role in fostering a positive and supportive work environment.

Enhances teamwork: Encouragement can enhance teamwork, as individuals feel supported and motivated to work together towards common goals.

Increases motivation: Encouragement can increase motivation, leading employees to work harder and strive for success.

Recognizes achievements: Encouragement through recognition of achievements can provide employees with a sense of accomplishment and fulfillment, promoting personal and professional growth.

Promotes open communication: Encouragement can promote open communication, as individuals feel comfortable expressing their thoughts and ideas in a supportive environment.

Supports professional development: Encouragement can support professional development, as individuals feel motivated to seek out new opportunities for growth and learning.

*Encouraging Success through Active listening and Empathy

Active listening involves demonstrating an understanding and awareness of the speaker by providing nonverbal cues (such as eye contact, nodding) as well as summarizing or reflecting what is being said. By listening to someone without interruption and without offering solutions, a person shows empathy and encourages the speaker to express themselves. Through active listening and empathy, a person can better understand the speaker's goals, challenges, and experiences, which in turn allows them to create more meaningful solutions and help them find success.

Encouraging success through active listening and empathy can lead to improved outcomes and overall success.

Supports understanding: Active listening and empathy allow individuals to understand the perspectives and needs of others, promoting a supportive and inclusive work environment.

Enhances communication: Active listening and empathy can enhance communication, as individuals feel heard and valued, leading to improved relationships and collaboration.

Promotes problem-solving: Active listening and empathy can promote effective problem-solving, as individuals feel heard and understood, leading to more creative and innovative solutions.

Increases motivation: Encouragement through active listening and empathy can increase motivation, as individuals feel valued and understood, leading to improved performance and productivity.

Supports continuous learning: Encouragement through active listening and empathy can support continuous learning, as individuals feel comfortable expressing their thoughts and ideas in a supportive environment.

Builds trust: Active listening and empathy can build trust, as individuals feel heard and understood, leading to improved relationships and collaboration.

*The importance of Encouraging Open Communication and Transparency

Encouraging open communication and transparency in the workplace is critical to an organization's success. Transparency fosters trust between employees, managers and customers, resulting in better relationships and an improved overall performance. Open communication creates an environment of collaboration, innovation, and creativity as it allows for different ideas to be shared and discussed. Additionally, open communication encourages dialogue and encourages problem-solving and goal-setting. Employees are able to openly share their concerns and provide valuable feedback to their supervisors, which can be used to shape the organization's strategy. Finally, transparency in the workplace increases job satisfaction and helps to attract and retain talented staff members. By fostering an open and honest work environment, companies can become more successful.

Encouraging open communication and transparency is important for several reasons.

Promotes trust: Open communication and transparency promote trust, as individuals feel heard and understood, leading to improved relationships and collaboration.

Supports problem-solving: Open communication and transparency can promote effective problem-solving, as individuals are able to openly discuss and address challenges.

Increases accountability: Encouraging open communication and transparency can increase accountability, as individuals are more likely to take ownership of their actions and responsibilities.

Enhances teamwork: Open communication and transparency can enhance teamwork, as individuals are able to openly discuss and coordinate their efforts towards common goals.

Promotes innovation: Encouraging open communication and transparency can promote innovation, as individuals are able to openly express their thoughts and ideas, leading to more creative and innovative solutions.

Supports personal and professional development: Encouraging open communication and transparency can support personal and professional development, as individuals feel comfortable expressing their thoughts and ideas in a supportive environment

*The Impact of Encouragement on Problem-Solving and Decision-Making

Encouragement has been proven to have a positive impact on problem-solving and decision-making. Studies have found that positive reinforcement leads to higher levels of engagement and increased effort, allowing for the processing of complex information. Individuals who receive encouragement tend to explore their options more thoroughly and view the available data from multiple angles. This, in turn, allows them to make informed decisions that they are confident in. Encouragement has also been shown to reduce stress and anxiety associated with problem-solving and decision-making, as it allows individuals to focus on the task without worrying about being judged or evaluated. Ultimately, receiving encouragement helps individuals approach problem-solving and decision-making more constructively, this can result in more creative solutions.

Encouragement has a positive effect on problem-solving and decision-making. When individuals feel encouraged, they tend to be more confident in their ability to solve problems and make decisions. This in turn leads to more creative problem-solving, as individuals are more willing to take risks and experiment with different ideas. Moreover, encouragement allows individuals to be more open to criticism, and it also helps them stay motivated throughout the decision-making process. Studies have found that individuals who receive positive feedback from peers or mentors are more likely to generate better ideas and solutions. Encouragement is also beneficial in that it can provide individuals with the psychological support and self-efficacy needed to persevere in the face of challenging situations. Thus, by creating a supportive and encouraging environment, organizations can improve their problem-solving and decision-making abilities.

*The Role of Encouragement in Fostering a Culture of Continuous Learning and Improvement

Encouragement is a vital factor in fostering a culture of continuous learning and improvement. Encouragement encourages learners to become more independent and confident, which can help them take ownership of their own learning. Furthermore, encouraging learners and recognizing their achievements, helps create an environment in which learners feel valued and can be motivated to achieve even greater results. Encouragement also helps build a collaborative and trusting culture in which learners can be open to trying new approaches and exploring new opportunities to advance their skills and knowledge. By offering frequent praise and recognizing even the smallest successes, learners will be more motivated to continue pushing the boundaries of their capabilities.

Encouragement is a powerful tool for fostering a culture of continuous learning and improvement. By acknowledging and praising positive behavior and progress, it serves to motivate people to strive for greater heights, as it highlights their efforts and encourages them to stay on track. Furthermore, encouraging messages that convey positive reinforcement and support can provide reassurance to those engaging in the learning process, as well as create a strong sense of accountability for meeting learning objectives. In this way, it provides both the individual and the organization with a sense of success. Ultimately, this reinforces a sense of ownership and commitment to continuing the learning process, which will encourage people to keep learning and continuously improve.

*How Can Encouragement Help you Succeed

Encouragement can help you succeed by boosting your confidence and motivation, making you feel supported and valued. It can also provide a positive outlook and help you overcome self-doubt, making it easier to persist through challenges and setbacks. Additionally, encouragement from others can help you identify your strengths and opportunities for improvement, leading to personal and professional growth.

*What are 10 Words that Bring you Inspiration

- Hope
- Dream
- Ambition
- Courage
- Gratitude
- Compassion
- Determination
- Empathy
- Resilience
- Positivity

*<u>What is the Value of Encouragement</u>

The value of encouragement is immense and can bring numerous benefits, including:

- Boosting confidence and motivation
- Providing support and reassurance
- Increasing resilience and perseverance
- Improving mental and emotional well-being
- Encouraging personal and professional growth
- Building relationships and fostering a positive community
- Providing a sense of belonging and self-worth
- Nurturing a growth mindset and positive self-image
- Helping to overcome challenges and setbacks
- Inspiring and motivating individuals to achieve their goals and aspirations.

*<u>Why is encouragement Important in Life</u>

Encouragement is important in life because it can have a profound impact on an individual's well-being and success. Some reasons why encouragement is important include:

- Boosting self-esteem and confidence
- Providing emotional support and motivation
- Encouraging personal and professional growth
- Overcoming challenges and setbacks
- Building relationships and fostering a positive community
- Nurturing a growth mindset and positive self-image
- Inspiring individuals to achieve their goals and aspirations
- Improving mental and emotional well-being
- Promoting resilience and perseverance
- Fostering a sense of belonging and self-worth.

Encouragement can come from various sources, including friends, family, colleagues, mentors, and even strangers, and can make a significant difference in an individual's life journey.

CHAPTER 4

*What is success through encouragement?

Success through encouragement is the concept that, in order to reach a goal, we need to be encouraged. We need to be reminded of why we are working on our goal and how great it will be once it is reached.

*Understanding the Power of Encouragement

Encouragement is a powerful force, and it has been shown to have a positive impact on a person's physical, mental and emotional health. Encouraging words also build trust and improve business relationships.

*Encouragement in the Workplace

Encouragement in the workplace is vital to employees' motivation. When employees feel supported and inspired, they'll be more likely to perform up to their best ability, both at work and at home.

Did you know that the way you show your appreciation of others can have a huge impact on your organizational culture? Try these tips to help cultivate an atmosphere of encouragement!

We all need a little encouragement sometimes, especially in the workplace where you can often feel alone and separate. When the team is down, it comes back up. When we are at our best, it will be there again tomorrow. When we don't feel like doing something, that little voice inside us knows what is best and encourages us to follow through with action. It's never too late to stop complaining and start saying "yes"

*Encouragement for personal growth

Encouragement for personal growth can help you in the road of life. Learning more is not only a human need but it helps to grow in a right direction and have a good future.

Sometimes, we need to be reminded that we're capable of doing more than what we believe. Encouragement for personal growth is a good way to remind ourselves of our potential, and should be heard and shared with others.

Encouragement is not a luxury, it's a necessity. Those who don't have supportive friends and family members do not survive. People that have the courage to follow their dreams are the ones that succeed in life. Encouragement can come from anyone and everywhere – your family, friends and even strangers.

If you want to be more successful at personal growth, work on emphasizing that it's okay to make mistakes, it's okay to feel uncomfortable and it's okay to feel that things are not going well. We all need to learn from our mistakes and experiences in order for us to grow and change. And the best way to do this is by practicing self-compassion! If you are having a rough day or if you've made a mistake, remind yourself that nobody is perfect, nobody has ever been perfect and there is nothing wrong with getting better or striving toward perfection!

*Encouragement in Relationships

Encouragement is the encouraging of someone to continue to make progress. Encouragement in relationships means to encourage others by helping them boost their confidence and strength.

Relationships are one of the most important things in our lives. And if you think about it, there's one very simple, but extremely powerful way to make sure your relationships stay strong: encouragement.

Encouragement in relationships is a forgotten or neglected aspect that has the power to change lives.

it is a really good book for people who want to be friends with their family members or wife/husband. It's very helpful to know how to talk to someone when you are in a relationship.

Encouragement in relationships is one of the main issues that people struggle with. We believe they need more encouragement, not less.

Encouragement in relationships is a great way to build trust between you and your partner. Encouraging others gives you a sense of control, knowing that someone else will be there for you when things go wrong. It can also help you deal with the ups and downs of life better.

Encouragement can help us to make the best choices, even in difficult circumstances. Encouraging someone -- or yourself with a "yes!" when you need it -- encourages us to try harder and see results. Encouragement is always present for anyone in need of help, especially those we love most. Be encouraging to others -- and yourself!

Relationships are difficult, and sometimes even scary. You can't always change the other person, but you can change yourself! Encouragement in relationships is about having confidence in your communication styles and loving yourself enough to give it to others.

Encouragement in relationships is vital for a healthy, successful relationship. It addresses the energy that exists between two people that is often influenced by the circumstances of our lives and what we think about ourselves. Encouraging yourself and others through positive affirmations are the key to using success as a catalyst for inspiration.

Improve your relationship with your spouse, family and friends through encouragement. Encourage one another as you face daily challenges and difficulties.

Encouragement in relationships can make a world of difference. In this episode, you'll hear from some of our Shoppers and experts about the importance of encouragement as a unifying force in your life with others.

*Encouragement for Children and Youth

Encouragement for children and youth is a way of encouraging them to be happy and to encourage them to do the right thing.

Encouragement is a powerful motivator which can help to develop a child's self-esteem, improve their confidence levels and promote positive choices.

I believe in the importance of being encouraged by the generosity of others. I would like to encourage people to give and help others. People don't need to be taught this lesson. It is more like a natural inclination within them if they are born with an open mind and a heart that wants to experience their life fully, i.e., develop, grow and flourish in their life.

Good morning, friends! How are you feeling today? Do you have a good attitude or are you wishing that something would change? This is a letter I wrote to my child, who was feeling bad about himself and the way he was acting. This letter helped him to feel better, and helped me to have a positive outlook on life.

Encouragement is a valid and important tool. Many times, encouragement has been shown to make a huge difference in someone's life. Encouragement can make a difference in how children and youth deal with everyday challenges as well as help them on their path to success. There are many ways you can encourage your children and youth by: - Support their dreams and aspirations - Show genuine interest in their lives - Recognize their strengths.

You are really important. If a child or youth have any needs, seek help from the people in your community. I am sure you will get what you need to be successful.

A strong attitude for children and youth is a key to their success, whether it's in academics, sports or personal lives. This is why we encourage building a positive self-esteem through encouragement from parents, family and teachers. Encouragement from a Grade 1 student can have such a domination impact on the future of that child that we must take extra care to create a positive environment for them at home and in school. From a very young age, children need to hear "I see you!" instead of "why do you always do that?"

Parents are the ones who raised your children, but you can't be a parent unless you belong to our community. You must always remember that when you help your child to grow up it also helps others in need. To build a better future for our children, we can all take part in making them feel inspired and motivated to reach their dreams!

*Encouragement in sports

Sports can be a challenging and competitive environment, but it can also be made more supportive and motivating through encouragement. Encouragement can come from many sources, such as coaches, teammates, family, or even self-encouragement. The power of encouragement lies in its ability to lift athletes up, boost their confidence, and help them overcome obstacles and reach their full potential.

Coaches play a significant role in providing encouragement in sports. By recognizing and praising athletes for their hard work and efforts, coaches can build their confidence and motivate them to perform at their best. They can also help athletes set and reach personal and team goals, and encourage continuous growth and development.

Teammates can also provide encouragement in sports. Whether it's through positive reinforcement, support during tough times, or helping each other reach their full potential, encouragement among teammates can foster a positive team dynamic, improve performance, and create a supportive and encouraging environment.

Encouragement can also play a crucial role in helping athletes overcome challenges and obstacles. Whether it's an injury, a loss, or simply a bad day, encouragement can provide the support and motivation needed to keep going and reach success.

Self-encouragement is also a vital aspect of success in sports. Athletes can boost their own confidence and motivation by setting goals, recognizing their strengths, and focusing on their achievements. This can help them overcome challenges, stay focused, and reach their full potential.

In conclusion, encouragement plays a significant role in sports and can make a positive impact on athletes and teams. By lifting athletes up, building their confidence, and providing support, encouragement can help individuals and teams reach their full potential and achieve success. Whether it's from coaches, teammates, family, or self-encouragement, success in sports is possible through encouragement and positivity.

*Encouragement in Education

Education can be a demanding and challenging journey, but it can also be made more achievable and enjoyable through encouragement. Encouragement can come from many sources, such as teachers, peers, parents, or even self-encouragement. The power of encouragement lies in its ability to lift students up, boost their confidence, and help them overcome obstacles and reach their full potential.

Teachers play a critical role in providing encouragement in education. By recognizing and praising students for their hard work and efforts, teachers can build their confidence and motivate them to perform at their best. They can also help students set and reach academic and personal goals, and encourage continuous learning and growth.

Peers can also provide encouragement in education. Whether it's through support during tough times, working together on projects, or helping each other reach their full potential, encouragement among peers can foster a positive learning environment, improve performance, and create supportive relationships.

Encouragement can also play a crucial role in helping students overcome challenges and obstacles. Whether it's a difficult subject, a low grade, or simply feeling overwhelmed, encouragement can provide the support and motivation needed to keep going and reach success.

Self-encouragement is also a vital aspect of success in education. Students can boost their own confidence and motivation by setting goals, recognizing their strengths, and focusing on their achievements. This can help them overcome challenges, stay focused, and reach their full potential.

In conclusion, encouragement plays a significant role in education and can make a positive impact on students and their learning journey. By lifting students up, building their confidence, and providing support, encouragement can help individuals reach their full potential and achieve success in their academic pursuits. Whether it's from teachers, peers, parents, or self-encouragement, success in education is possible through encouragement and positivity.

*Encouragement for Those Facing Challenges

Challenges are a part of life and can range from minor setbacks to major obstacles. Regardless of the size of the challenge, it can be difficult to overcome and remain motivated. However, encouragement can play a crucial role in helping individuals facing challenges to overcome them and reach success.

Encouragement can come from many sources, such as friends, family, mentors, or even self-encouragement. The power of encouragement lies in its ability to lift individuals up, boost their confidence, and provide support in times of need. Encouragement can help individuals overcome challenges by giving them the motivation and strength they need to keep going.

For those facing major challenges, such as illness or injury, encouragement can play a critical role in helping them stay positive and motivated. Whether it's through words of encouragement, acts of kindness, or simply being there to listen, encouragement can help individuals facing challenges to keep their spirits high and maintain their focus on recovery and success.

Self-encouragement is also an important aspect for those facing challenges. Individuals can boost their own confidence and motivation by setting goals, recognizing their strengths, and focusing on their achievements. This can help them overcome challenges, stay focused, and reach their full potential.

In conclusion, encouragement is a powerful tool for those facing challenges. By lifting individuals up, building their confidence, and providing support, encouragement can help individuals overcome obstacles and reach success. Whether it's from friends, family, mentors, or self-encouragement, success is possible through encouragement and positivity, even in the face of challenges.

*<u>The importance of self-encouragement</u>

Self-encouragement is a vital aspect of personal growth and success. It involves recognizing and praising one's own efforts, abilities, and achievements, and providing oneself with motivation and support. Self-encouragement is a powerful tool that can help individuals overcome obstacles, boost their confidence, and reach their full potential.

Self-encouragement helps individuals to focus on their strengths and abilities, rather than dwelling on their weaknesses. By recognizing their achievements and focusing on their progress, individuals can maintain a positive outlook and stay motivated, even in the face of challenges. This can help individuals to maintain their confidence, overcome obstacles, and achieve their goals.

Self-encouragement also helps individuals to develop resilience and determination. By providing themselves with support and motivation, individuals can stay focused on their goals and push through tough times, which can lead to long-term success. This can also help individuals to develop a growth mindset, where they see challenges as opportunities for growth and development, rather than as insurmountable obstacles.

In addition, self-encouragement can help individuals to maintain their self-esteem and well-being. By focusing on their positive qualities and abilities, individuals can build a strong sense of self-worth and maintain their confidence and motivation. This can lead to a more fulfilling and enjoyable life, as well as improved performance in personal and professional pursuits.

In conclusion, self-encouragement is a critical aspect of personal growth and success. By providing individuals with motivation and support, self-encouragement can help individuals overcome obstacles, boost their confidence, and reach their full potential. By recognizing and praising their own efforts and abilities, individuals can maintain a positive outlook, build resilience, and develop a growth mindset, leading to a more fulfilling and successful life.

*Encouragement and motivation

Encouragement and motivation are concepts that refer to inspiring and driving individuals to achieve their goals. Encouragement involves offering support and positive reinforcement to individuals to boost their confidence and self-esteem, while motivation refers to the internal drive that pushes a person to act in a certain way.

Encouragement can come from various sources such as family, friends, teachers, coaches, and mentors. It can be expressed through verbal or non-verbal affirmations, recognition of accomplishments, and providing constructive feedback.

Motivation, on the other hand, can stem from various factors such as personal interests, desires, and needs. It can be intrinsic, meaning it comes from within, or extrinsic, meaning it comes from external factors such as rewards or punishments.

Both encouragement and motivation play a crucial role in personal and professional growth and development. They help individuals overcome challenges, persist through difficult times, and reach their full potential.

*Encouragement in leadership

Encouragement is indeed an important aspect of leadership. A leader should recognize and celebrate the successes of their followers, and when something is done incorrectly, the leader should focus on the solution rather than blaming or shaming their followers. Furthermore, leaders should give frequent positive reinforcement in order to foster motivation and inspiration in the people they lead. Doing this helps to boost morale, create loyalty and build team cohesion. Overall, when a leader can combine criticism and praise effectively, it can help to bring out the best in their followers and create an atmosphere of motivation and support.

Boost morale and motivation: Encouragement from a leader can help team members feel valued and appreciated, which can in turn increase their motivation to perform at their best.

Foster teamwork: Encouraging words and a positive attitude from a leader can help build trust and cohesion among team members, promoting a sense of shared purpose and collaboration.

Improve performance: Encouragement can help team members set and reach their goals, and can provide the support they need to overcome obstacles and challenges.

Develop potential: Leaders who encourage their team members can help them identify their strengths and weaknesses and develop their skills, leading to increased personal and professional growth.

*Encouragement and Positive Reinforcement

Encouragement and positive reinforcement are an essential part of effective teaching and learning. When students are given positive reinforcement, it can help build self-esteem and motivate them to try harder and put in extra effort. When students are given positive reinforcement, it shows them that their efforts are valued and that their accomplishments are worth celebrating. Encouragement can be verbal or nonverbal. Examples of verbal encouragement could be telling the student that they did a great job or providing them with words of affirmation. Examples of nonverbal reinforcement could include clapping or giving high-fives after completing a task. Positive reinforcement should be provided in a timely manner, as students respond better when their achievements are rewarded in a timely fashion. Overall, providing students with encouragement and positive reinforcement helps them stay engaged, learn more, and be more confident.

Encouragement and positive reinforcement can help to motivate and encourage individuals to achieve their goals. Encouraging and positive reinforcement involves recognizing an individual for their hard work, effort and successes, as well as praising and reinforcing the behavior which lead to successes. This helps individuals feel empowered and supported in their endeavors. Positive reinforcement can also include verbal, physical, or symbolic rewards such as praise, gifts, and tokens of recognition. These methods of positive reinforcement will help individuals feel valued and appreciated, while providing the incentive and motivation needed to succeed.

Encouragement and positive reinforcement are essential for helping a student develop confidence, enthusiasm, and resilience. Encouraging words, compliments, rewards, and praise are all effective tools for boosting self-esteem and fostering positive growth in a student. Creating meaningful and rewarding experiences that a student enjoys, celebrating successes and accomplishments, and providing feedback on improvement are all important strategies for helping a student develop positive attributes. It's also important to provide constructive feedback when a student does not reach their goals, as this can provide them with the motivation and support needed to strive for excellence.

Encouragement and positive reinforcement are two tools that are used in behavior management and training. Encouragement involves praising, recognizing, or reinforcing desired behaviors and actions with verbal approval and positive reinforcement, such as rewards. Positive reinforcement is providing an incentive for desired behavior, such as providing a reward, or making an individual feel appreciated for the actions taken. Encouragement and positive reinforcement can both be used in the classroom, at work, or in any environment to promote desired behaviors. By consistently reinforcing desired behaviors, individuals are more likely to engage in those activities, leading to increased productivity and more effective results.

*Encouragement and accountability

Encouragement and accountability are important for any relationship to be successful. Encouragement is about building a person up and recognizing their strengths and successes. It's about being positive and motivating them to continue striving for the best. Accountability involves being open and honest, expecting and accepting responsibility and ownership, and showing integrity and reliability. This is key to developing a sense of trust in any relationship. When a person is held accountable, they are more likely to stay on track and achieve their goals. Both encouragement and accountability are needed to build and sustain any type of relationship.

Encouragement and accountability can go hand in hand in order to promote healthy and effective behavior. Encouragement is essential for instilling motivation and providing positive reinforcement, which is needed for learning and development. At the same time, accountability can be used to provide additional incentives for sticking to commitments and for creating and maintaining progress. The key to creating an effective environment of encouragement and accountability is to ensure that rewards are paired with constructive feedback and that failure to reach goals is seen as an opportunity to grow and develop. By establishing clear goals and expectations and then reinforcing these with a mixture of praise and criticism, individuals can be held to high standards while still feeling appreciated and valued.

Encouragement and accountability are both important elements in the development of any successful team. Encouragement should focus on recognizing individual achievements and praising team efforts. Additionally, managers should create a supportive environment by fostering open dialogue, enabling feedback and providing positive reinforcement.

Accountability is equally important and can help to reinforce good behaviors and foster improvement. Team members should be expected to adhere to agree upon standards, complete their tasks and help others reach their goals. Clear goals and expectations should be established to ensure that team members understand the tasks at hand and are held to a reasonable level of accountability. If goals are not met, teams should discuss how they could have achieved a better result, providing valuable learning and experience for the future.

Encouragement and accountability are essential components for successful change. Providing support and offering words of encouragement can help motivate someone to work hard and stay committed to their goal. Setting regular check-ins and having someone who holds you accountable can also be useful to stay on track and be held responsible for achieving desired outcomes. Working together in this way can help create and maintain healthy habits, focus, and discipline in order to reach any given goal.

Encouragement and accountability go hand-in-hand when trying to motivate and support someone. Encouragement is about recognizing and rewarding efforts and progress, whereas accountability is about making sure goals are met and reminding someone when tasks are not done. Together, they create an environment where success can be achieved.

*Encouragement and perseverance

Encouragement and perseverance are two key elements to any success story. Having people around you to encourage you to reach for the stars can be just as powerful as working hard and putting in the extra effort. Encouragement is essential when facing difficult situations, or just as a reminder to never give up on yourself. When feeling discouraged, it's important to remember that failure can be just as important as success, as it often leads to personal growth. Persistence and dedication are also key elements to any success story. Dedication is often the driving force behind achieving one's goals and reaching milestones. Keeping up the hard work and determination will help you stay on the path of success. When combined with encouragement, dedication, and perseverance will result in the desired success.

Encouragement and perseverance are two of the most important qualities needed to achieve success. Encouragement provides motivation to take the first step and continue moving forward, while perseverance provides the commitment and determination to stay the course no matter what. Both of these qualities must work together to make progress and attain the desired goal. It's important to remember that everyone's journey to success looks different, so patience and acceptance are key components as well. Encouragement and perseverance should be used as tools to help make positive change and accomplish your goals.

Encouragement and perseverance are essential for anyone who is attempting to achieve a goal or embark on a new project. Encouragement gives people the energy and motivation to keep going and persevere. With encouragement and support, a person is more likely to believe in their own abilities and continue trying until they have succeeded. Similarly, perseverance allows a person to remain focused and motivated even in the face of adversity. With dedication and tenacity, a person can keep pushing towards their goals, even if they face challenges along the way. Together, encouragement and perseverance are powerful tools that help to make any challenge a bit easier to conquer.

*Encourage others to succeed

1. **Never underestimate the power of positivity.** You all know how big a believer I am of the power of positivity! When you're someone who's truly dedicated to leading and supporting others to bring out their best, you radiate positivity and sincerity. Coaching often involves giving feedback, and we're all much more receptive when feedback is coming from a positive place rather than a negative one! Positivity is also infectious, so you'll be brightening up the whole workplace too!

2. **Develop real relationships and build trust.** Just because you're the leader doesn't mean your team automatically trusts you. Trust is something that must be

earned, and the best way to do this is by treating your team as more than just numbers – get to know each person individually, and find out their goals and motivators. By showing a genuine interest in your team as people, you're demonstrating that you're a leader who's focused on others, not just themselves. This will build your teams' trust in you and allow you all to work together much more effectively.

3. **Use SMART goal setting**. The SMART goal setting technique is fantastic. It's one of my favourite coaching and performance tools, and I recommend any leader worth their salt use it regularly. SMART stands for Specific, Measurable, Attainable, Relevant and Time-Based, all of which are pretty self-explanatory. Giving your goals a clear structure and breaking them down into smaller and more achievable goals ensures a higher chance of success – introduce it to your team if you haven't already, and see the difference it makes!

4. **Give (and ask for) feedback**. Regular feedback helps keep everyone on track and identifies issues before they turn into bigger problems, as well as providing motivation and encouragement. You'll also identify any knowledge gaps or training that's required, and find out if there are any other resources your team feels they may need to better achieve the results you're after. It's important to remember that great leaders don't just give constructive and helpful feedback, they ask for it as well. How can you improve and get better if you aren't getting anyone else's point of view?

5. **Use open-ended, not closed, questions**. While you can't always avoid the 'yes' or 'no' questions, you need to make sure the bulk of your questioning is made up of open-ended questions so that you can encourage others to share their feelings and thoughts in more detail. You'll be able to identify what needs improving, as well as current attitudes and whether everyone understands what needs to be done.

6. **Promote transparency**. Transparency is another way to build trust and foster open communication and to make sure that everyone is on the same page. Transparency helps form and maintain relationships, and encourages consistency. By being open about your own journey, you're showing your team that you are relatable and not infallible – dismantling the 'leaders must be perfect and never wrong' stereotype is vital to building positive employee relationships. Demonstrating openness encourages those around you to do the same and allows you to lead by example, which is a much more effective way to lead than the old 'do as I say, not as I do' way of thinking.

CHAPTER 5

*Encouragement and Resilience

Individuals need resilience to achieve success, so it is necessary to encourage them to become resilient and endure. Encouragement from others may spur you to continue working hard in the face of adversity and persevere to see a project through to the end. Encouragement can come in many different forms, like giving verbal approval, giving constructive feedback, or when someone makes you feel better about yourself by talking positively about something you have accomplished. Verbal approval is what we say about you, for example, to build your self-confidence or motivate you. Constructive feedback is a helpful thing to get because it shows where you can get better and also what areas of your life to improve on. No matter what the shape it takes, encouragement will give you the motivation to go on through tough moments and to attain new levels of success. You also have to keep in mind that you can give yourself the same encouragement that others would give to you. It's important to take time every day to affirm your self-worth and recognize what you've accomplished, and even if it sounds self-involved or odd at first, be persistent with this kind of self-encouragement; it'll only bring good results. As a whole, encouragement and resilience are two of the most important elements for success. While encouragement from others can motivate us to reach for our goals, self-encouragement can ground and keep us focused on them. With these two strengths at our disposal, we will have the confidence and strength we need to take on anything we might confront in life.

*Encouragement and Emotional well-being

When it comes to success, encouragement is one of the key ingredients for achieving it. It can provide a much-needed boost of motivation and confidence that helps us to overcome challenges and strive for our goals. Encouragement, whether from a mentor, a coach, or even a friend, can go a long way in helping us stay focused and resilient during difficult times.

Encouragement also has an emotional component to it. It can serve to validate us, build self-esteem, and provide the necessary reassurance to take risks and make positive changes. In addition to providing motivation and inspiration, it can help us to move forward despite setbacks or failure. By being able to accept failure as part of the journey rather than as an end-all, it's easier to persevere and succeed in the long run.

Not only can encouragement help to propel us towards success, but it can also help us maintain our emotional well-being. A supportive environment is essential for personal growth and happiness, and encouragement from others can serve as a powerful reminder of our own capabilities and potential. It can help us gain the courage to take on challenges and face our fears with a sense of optimism and resilience. Furthermore, feeling appreciated and validated can also help to reduce stress and anxiety.

In conclusion, encouragement plays an essential role in achieving success as well as maintaining emotional well-being. It can provide a valuable source of motivation and assurance that allows us to confront our challenges and make progress towards our goals. Ultimately, encouragement can be a powerful tool for personal growth and development, so it's important to take the time to give and receive it.

*Encouragement and Stress Management

Encouragement is an extremely effective technique for obtaining achievement. It inspires and motivates us, allowing us to achieve our objectives. It can help relieve stress by providing encouragement to keep going even when things get tough. According to research, persons who receive encouragement from family, friends, and colleagues are more likely to succeed than those who do not. Knowing how to provide constructive criticism is one of the most critical parts of good encouraging. Rather to merely telling someone they're doing well, offer concrete, tangible suggestions for how they might improve.For example, if a colleague is having difficulty with a project, make suggestions on how they might better organize their time or approach the issue in a different way.

Encouragement is more than just giving compliments; it is also about offering emotional support. Assure your loved ones that you are always available to them and that you will listen when they need someone to talk to. This type of emotional support can be especially beneficial when confronted with challenging situations or decisions. It is also crucial to help regulate stress levels in addition to offering emotional support.The trick here is to strike a balance between pushing yourself and looking after your emotional health. Take frequent pauses from work, get enough sleep, and exercise on a regular basis. Taking time for yourself will help relieve stress and provide you with the energy to face any challenges that may arise. Encouragement and stress management are two crucial components of success. You can set yourself up for success and overcome any obstacles that come your way if you have the correct attitude, support system, and self-care routines.

*Encouragement and positive attitude

It is often said that success comes to those who work hard and never give up, but it also takes more than hard work alone to achieve success. Encouragement and positive attitude can play a big part in reaching your goals.

Encouragement is a powerful tool that can provide the motivation and drive to push through tough times and reach success. It can be something as small as a simple comment or an act of kindness that can boost someone's confidence and make them feel more determined to continue working hard.

Positive attitude is also very important in achieving success. Having a positive outlook on life will help you stay focused on your goals and keep going when things get tough. It's easy to become discouraged and give up, but having a positive attitude will help you stay on track and see the opportunities even in the most difficult of times.

Finally, don't forget to take care of yourself. Your health and well-being are essential for staying motivated and continuing to make progress. Set aside time each day to relax, unwind, and recharge your batteries. Taking care of yourself is just as important as working hard towards success.

Encouragement and positive attitude are key components in reaching success. Making the effort to be encouraging and maintain a positive attitude can have a huge impact on achieving your goals. So take the time to nurture yourself and those around you, and enjoy the rewards of your hard work.

*Encouragement and time management

These two topics are critical for success, but often overlooked. Encouragement helps you stay motivated and focused on reaching your goals while time management helps to ensure that you use the limited time you have efficiently and effectively. When combined, they create a powerful tool to help you achieve your goals. Encouragement is essential for success because it can keep you motivated and focused on the task at hand. It can be difficult to stay motivated and focused in the face of adversity, especially if you don't have anyone around to encourage and motivate you. That's why it's important to give yourself positive feedback and encouragement throughout the process. Whether it's taking a break when you're feeling overwhelmed or celebrating small successes, finding ways to reward yourself for your hard work can be incredibly beneficial in staying motivated and focused.

Time management is equally as important for success. With limited time in the day, it's important to prioritize tasks and manage your time effectively in order to maximize efficiency and productivity. Developing good habits such as creating to-do lists, breaking down tasks into smaller chunks, and setting realistic deadlines can help make sure that all of your important tasks get done in a timely manner. Additionally, learning to say "no" to activities that aren't productive or important can help you manage your time better. Overall, both encouragement and time management are essential elements for success. Through encouraging yourself to stay motivated and managing your time effectively, you can make sure that you're making progress towards your goals and achieving the success that you desire.

*Encouragement and communication skills

Encouragement and communication skills are essential for achieving success in any pursuit. Encouragement is a crucial component of a successful team, both in the business and in personal relationships. Learning how to properly inspire and motivate others is a crucial ability for everyone trying to advance in life.

Encouragement doesn't have to be complicated or extravagant. It can be as easy as giving someone a pat on the back after they've done something properly or paying close attention to them while they're attempting to explain an issue.It's also important to give sincere compliments when they have achieved something or done a good job. This will help them feel appreciated and valued, which can have a powerful effect on their motivation and willingness to take risks.

Good communication skills are also essential for success. People need to be able to communicate effectively with their colleagues and bosses, as well as with their customers, clients, and partners. Good communication can mean the difference between success and failure.

Having good communication skills involves more than just speaking; it also includes listening, understanding, and being able to articulate ideas and opinions clearly. Being able to ask meaningful questions and provide helpful feedback can make all the difference in how well people can work together towards achieving a goal. Encouragement and communication skills are both essential elements of success, no matter what field or area you are working in. Whether you are working in the corporate world or managing a home, having these skills will help you stay focused, motivated, and successful.

*Encouragement and Problem-Solving

Family, friends, colleagues and even yourself can encourage you to reach your goals in life and in business. Staying motivated is crucial to achieving your goals. Supporting someone to reach their goals is not only important but also highly effective when it comes to success. It helps them feel valued and appreciated, which leads to increased performance and engagement. When someone is encouraged to keep going regardless of obstacles, they are more likely to stay focused and determined. Identifying problems, developing solutions, and acting on them are essential skills for success in any field. To find the right solution, you should be creative, organized, and systematic, as well as taking feedback from others into consideration; finding solutions that would otherwise go unnoticed can be made easier with a second opinion. As a result, both encouragement and problem-solving are crucial elements of success. Encouragement helps people stay motivated and determined, while problem-solving allows them to come up with creative solutions that can lead to success. It is possible to achieve your goals by combining these two approaches.

*Encouragement and Creativity

It is commonly stated that success begins with encouragement. Encouragement may come from a variety of sources, including family and friends, instructors, mentors, and peers. Everyone requires encouragement from time to time, and it may make a significant impact in our lives.

Encouragement is essential for releasing creativity and assisting us in reaching our greatest potential. When we receive encouragement, we are able to explore our creative side and develop new ideas and solutions that can lead to success. It also motivates us to take chances, since when someone believes in us, we are more willing to attempt something new.The significance of encouragement cannot be overstated. A little encouragement may go a long way, and it's necessary for every successful endeavour. Having someone who believes in you gives you the confidence and bravery to take on new challenges and have faith that you can achieve great things. Encouragement is also vital in maintaining motivation levels. Being encouraged helps us stay focused on our goals and keep moving forward, especially when the going gets rough. Knowing that someone is there to support us is vital and may be the difference between success and failure.Finally, encouragement and creativity are essential parts of success. Encouragement allows us to express ourselves creatively, take chances, and stay motivated. It's a priceless resource that can make a significant difference in anyone's life.

*Encouragement and innovation

We all need a little encouragement now and then, and it's no different when it comes to attaining success. Encouragement from others may be quite helpful in achieving our objectives since it can give us the boost we need to be motivated and keep going.

Success also requires innovation. It's critical to push ourselves and come up with fresh ideas to assist us achieve our goals faster and more efficiently. Taking the effort to look outside the box and create fresh issue solutions may go a long way.It is essential for success to find the correct balance of encouragement and innovation. It may take some trial and error, but by pushing ourselves and asking questions on a regular basis, we can uncover fresh chances that will help us achieve our goals. As we continue to look for answers, we may come across ones we hadn't considered previously!Encouragement and innovation are two important factors that might assist us on our path to success. They can provide us the inspiration and inventiveness we need to move forward and achieve our objectives. So, don't be hesitant to seek support from others around you, and take the time to devise novel answers to any problems you may face. With the correct mix of both, you'll be well on your way to reaching your objectives in no time!

*<u>Encouragement and Learning</u>

Encouragement is a strong tool for helping people achieve their objectives and develop. When we are encouraged and applauded for our achievements, it inspires us to keep going and strive for more. It is an essential component of self-improvement and growth. The process of developing information and abilities via experience is known as learning. It entails acquiring new information and using that knowledge in practical ways.

Individuals may make significant strides in their growth by combining encouragement and learning. Encouragement gives the motivation and emotional support required to learn and <u>develop new abilities. Learning provides us with the tools and approaches to put our newly</u> gained talents to use.

Encouragement also helps others learn more successfully. It fosters a good atmosphere in which individuals may make errors and try new things without fear of being criticized or mocked. This environment encourages children to develop confidence in their talents and to be more creative in their approaches to learning. Encouragement of one another fosters teamwork and problem-solving. People who are encouraged to communicate their ideas and cooperate on assignments are more likely to come up with innovative solutions than those who work alone. This sort of collaborative learning pushes people to think outside the box and devise creative solutions.

Encouragement combined with learning is a strong instrument for personal growth and development. We can assist create an environment of learning and progress for everyone engaged by encouraging and providing feedback to one another. Furthermore, encouraging one another to learn new skills and gain information allows us to remain ahead of the competition and keep up with the ever-changing world around us.

CHAPTER 6

*Encouragement and personal development

Encouragement and personal development go hand in hand. It is an integral part of being successful and reaching one's potential. Encouragement not only boosts confidence, but it helps people reach their goals and encourages them to take action.

One way to foster growth and progress is through positive reinforcement. Praising a person's efforts and achievements can be a powerful motivator that spurs them to do more. Acknowledging the successes, however small, provides recognition and builds self-esteem. Additionally, giving specific feedback on what went right or what could be improved helps develop skills and build on strengths. It is also important to set realistic expectations and provide feedback throughout the journey. Giving feedback at appropriate times helps guide individuals and keeps them on track. It shows that you believe in their capabilities and can provide the motivation needed to achieve their goals.

Encouragement should be tailored to the individual. Everyone responds differently to encouragement, so it is essential to find out what works for each person. Some may thrive off recognition, while others might require constructive criticism. Finding the right balance of praise and feedback can help maximize the chances of success.

In addition to offering verbal encouragement, providing tangible incentives can be extremely motivating. Offering rewards or prizes, such as gift cards or time off, can help keep individuals on task and encourage progress.

When it comes to personal development, goal setting is a must. Setting specific goals and breaking them into manageable pieces helps break large tasks down into smaller steps and creates actionable plans that can be tracked.

Finally, a supportive environment is key to fostering growth and progress. Surrounding yourself with like-minded people who are striving for similar goals can help keep you motivated and focused on achieving success.

Encouragement and personal development are intertwined processes that can be used to create positive changes in our lives. They provide motivation, guidance, and incentive for growth and progress. With the right tools and support, anyone can achieve great success through encouragement and personal development.

*Encouragement and professional development

Encouragement is an essential component of professional and personal success. When confronted with everyday obstacles and disappointments, it may be tough to remain motivated at work, but encouragement can help keep people on track and make them more productive.

Encouragement may help workers improve professionally in addition to offering inspiration and positive reinforcement. When team members are encouraged to take on new duties or responsibilities, their skill set grows and they become more valued members of the team. It also fosters a culture of trust and cooperation, which aids in the development of relationships and fosters a feeling of belonging in the workplace.

Managers and supervisors benefit from encouragement as well. When team members are encouraged to venture outside of their comfort zone and take on challenges, it demonstrates that the manager believes in them and wants to see them succeed. This may be really motivating for staff and make the management appear excellent!

Finally, supporting professional growth may aid in the recruitment of brilliant new personnel. When existing team members are given the opportunity to grow and develop, it demonstrates to prospective workers that the organization is committed to assisting its employees in progressing and reaching their full potential. This might help a company stand out in a crowded employment market. Overall, team performance is dependent on encouragement and professional growth. Managers and supervisors may create an atmosphere in which team members can flourish and achieve by encouraging staff to take on challenges and improve professionally.

*Encouragement and change management

Encouragement is an essential component in change management. When done effectively, it may deliver a significant boost to morale and productivity. To get the most out of this strategy, you must first grasp what it is, how to use it, and how to avoid frequent mistakes. What exactly is encouragement?

Encouragement is a kind of positive reinforcement in which individuals and teams are supported, acknowledged, and recognized for their achievements. It is a means to show appreciation and thanks, as well as to create trust and teamwork. Encouragement's goal is to create a stimulating atmosphere in which individuals feel appreciated and encouraged to take on difficulties.

When employed as part of a change management process, encouragement may give vital support to team members during times of transition. The emphasis should be on recognizing outstanding work, celebrating triumphs, and offering relevant feedback and assistance.

Leaders may motivate their staff by establishing clear objectives, setting attainable goals, providing assistance, and praising a job well done. Managers should also attempt to develop an environment of open communication and cooperation in order to build a feeling of camaraderie and togetherness.

It's critical to remember that motivation should be a continuous effort throughout the change management process. It should also be adapted to individual team members' demands, since everyone has distinct requirements.

Encouragement may quickly become overpowering. When provided too regularly or in the wrong way, it may foster reliance or even anger. Furthermore, encouragement should never be used as a substitute for constructive criticism or as a reward for failure. Encouragement is a critical component of good change management. Leaders may give essential assistance to their teams during times of change if they understand how to utilize it effectively. However, it is critical to utilize encouragement wisely in order to prevent developing a culture of reliance or resentment. Encouragement, when utilized correctly, may help teams remain motivated and focused on achievement.

*Encouragement and conflict resolution

Encouragement is a strong tool that may assist individuals in reaching their objectives and achieving success. It's a method of thanking someone for their hard work and showing them that you believe in them. Simultaneously, it may aid in the reduction of conflict between people and groups, enabling them to collaborate in a more effective and peaceful way.

There are numerous crucial factors to consider while delivering encouragement. First and foremost, it is critical to deliver good comments and convey gratitude. This contributes to the development of an atmosphere of mutual respect and trust, which is necessary for effective cooperation.

It's also crucial to consider how you frame your words of encouragement. Positive phrases such as "you did fantastic!" or "I'm very proud of you!" may have a significant influence on the recipient's drive and confidence. Avoid using harsh words, since this might have the opposite impact.

Furthermore, sincere appreciation and praise for others is a great approach to motivate others. People sometimes feel unappreciated in their daily lives, therefore praising their contributions may be quite rewarding.

Finally, it is critical to stay cool and impartial while resolving conflicts. Listen carefully to all sides of the narrative, give everyone a chance to express themselves without interruption, and search for common ground. It is simpler to find a mutually beneficial solution when all sides understand each other.

Encouragement and conflict resolution are inextricably linked. It is possible to go ahead in a productive and constructive way by offering positive reinforcement and attentively listening to other opinions.

*Encouragement and decision making

If you're having trouble with your decisions, try to remember that a big part of success is trusting ourselves and having confidence in our abilities. One of the most helpful things for motivating ourselves is support. Support can come from both from within or from the people around us. Encouragement enables us to concentrate on the final result and conquer any barriers to getting there. It empowers us to have faith in ourselves and to feel strong enough to take on any challenges. We also learn from it and take with us a sense of self-assurance in being able to make smart decisions and being receptive to different outcomes. When we're encouraged by other people, it's easier to think outside the box. We feel empowered to take chances and try new things because we know that, no matter the outcome, there is always somebody's help, their acceptance, and a net to catch us when we inevitably fall. Positive relationships with supportive individuals is a critical factor in self-motivation. Finally, encouragement is an important factor in the decisions that we make. When we are provided with support and affirmation, we are able to explore the different options available to us and we are able to make decisions that can truly be beneficial for us. The best sources of encouragement may not be close to you or know you well but support, even coming from strangers, is necessary for achievement.

*Encouragement and Teamwork

Encouragement and teamwork are important components of success. When we encourage and support one another in our objectives, we create an environment of development and success. Working together with a positive mindset may help us achieve our objectives more quickly and successfully.

Encouragement is essential for increasing morale and developing trust among a team. This may be accomplished by simply saying words of encouragement like "excellent job" or "keep up the good work." Individual achievements should also be recognized since they may assist boost team spirit.

Teamwork is also a crucial aspect of success. Teamwork include not just individuals working together, but also how they connect with one another. Teams may function more efficiently and successfully if they understand each other's responsibilities and talents. Teamwork may also promote cooperation, problem solving, and the creation of an atmosphere in which everyone feels appreciated.

Finally, remember that everyone is essential and that everyone has something useful to offer the team. Everyone, regardless of job, has something to give. Each individual has distinct abilities and talents that should be acknowledged and valued. We can assist create a workplace where everyone feels appreciated and valued by cultivating an attitude of gratitude and happiness.

Encouragement and collaboration are critical success factors. We can build a successful team that can achieve big things by creating a supportive atmosphere, acknowledging individual successes, and respecting everyone's efforts.

*Encouragement and Productivity

Encouragement is a powerful tool that may be utilized to help people achieve their objectives and become more productive. Encouragement is not only a kind of support and encouragement, but it can also be a powerful motivator for people to accomplish their goals.

When encouraging others, it is critical to emphasize the good parts of their performance rather than delivering criticism or reprimands. Individuals are more inclined to take on jobs with excitement and energy when they are given encouraging words and comments. Encouragement may come in both vocal and nonverbal forms. For example, you may use phrases like "excellent work" or "I believe in you" to encourage others. Nonverbal encouragement might take the form of a pat on the back or an embrace.

Encouragement should also be given in a timely way. If someone is working hard and producing good outcomes, recognize their efforts as soon as feasible. This will assist to reinforce the desirable behavior and motivate them to try more in the future.

It's also vital to keep track of how often you provide words of encouragement. Excessive praise might lose its significance and perhaps lead to complacency or a false feeling of security. It is preferable to provide particular appreciation for specific activities or results rather than general praise for everything.

Finally, while encouraging others, be certain that the praise is real and true. People can sense if someone is merely saying something because they think they should, so offer real praises and words of encouragement from the heart.

Encouragement may be a powerful motivator and has been related to increased productivity. You may establish a supportive atmosphere that motivates folks to strive for success by being careful of how you express encouragement.

*<u>Encouragement and Effective Delegation</u>

The ability to inspire and encourage their staff is the key to success for every leader. It is important to acknowledge that each person has distinct skills and shortcomings. As a leader, you must consider these distinctions and modify your approach to meet the requirements of each individual.

Encouragement and delegating are two of the most effective methods to do this. When a team member succeeds, positive reinforcement is given, and constructive criticism is given when they make errors. This contributes to the development of trust and understanding between the leader and their team, which is necessary for effective cooperation.

Delegation, on the other hand, is allocating particular duties to various team members depending on their skills and shortcomings. You can increase productivity and guarantee that everyone is working toward the same objective by delegating duties to the correct individuals.

Encouragement and delegating are critical techniques for any leader seeking to cultivate a productive and successful team. You may foster a successful culture in your firm by recognizing individual abilities, offering positive reinforcement, and distributing duties effectively.

*<u>Encouragement and Mentorship</u>

It is important to have support, advice, and encouragement in any successful endeavor. Whether you're a corporate leader, entrepreneur, or student, the assistance of mentors and peers may be invaluable in achieving your objectives.

Encouragement allows us to stay focused on our objectives and provides us the confidence to pursue them. It might come from people around us, such as friends and family, or it can originate from inside ourselves. Self-encouragement is the most significant kind of encouragement since it increases our drive and dedication to achieving our goals.

Mentorship is also an important factor in obtaining success. Mentors may provide advise and direction, share their own experiences, and link us with resources to help us achieve our objectives. Mentors may also inspire us by demonstrating what is possible. Finding a mentor who can guide us through tough times and push us to take on new challenges is priceless.

Success needs both encouragement and guidance. They inspire us to persevere when circumstances are difficult and remind us of our immense potential. We are better prepared to face any situation now that we have these two resources at our disposal.

*Encouragement and Networking

Encouragement and networking are often used to pave the way to success. Encouragement may be a great motivator for yourself and others to achieve their objectives. It is critical to acknowledge when someone has accomplished something or made progress toward a goal, and to encourage them to keep going. Positive feedback and acknowledgment of accomplishments may help drive individuals to keep working hard.

Networking is also essential for success. Building connections and contacts may provide you with resources, guidance, and opportunities that you would not have otherwise. It is important to connect with others who share your interests and ambitions. Connecting with coworkers, mentors, and other experts in your sector might be part of this. Having counsel and assistance from these relationships may help you achieve your objectives.

When striving for success, keep in mind that although development is not always constant, continuous effort and attention will pay off in the end. Surrounding yourself with good individuals who will encourage and support you can help you stay motivated and on track.

*Encouragement and Continuous Improvement

Encouragement is vital for success. It is essential for keeping individuals motivated and on track with their objectives. Encouragement helps to enhance confidence and motivation when confronted with difficulties or barriers. In the quest of success, continuous development is also essential. This entails defining quantifiable objectives and working hard to achieve them. It entails being open to learning and developing, being aware of errors, and taking remedial action.

Positive behaviors, attitudes, and actions are recognized and reinforced via encouragement. Depending on the circumstances, it might be offered directly or indirectly. For example, you may say something like, "I'm proud of you for working so hard!" or "Well done for doing something out of your comfort zone!" These are excellent approaches to encourage and recognize someone's accomplishments.

Tools such as project management systems and goal-setting activities may help to foster continuous development. Project management tools enable you to monitor progress and assess achievement in real time, while goal-setting activities help you create realistic goals and stay focused. There are also several tools accessible to assist you in your continuous improvement journey, such as tutorials, webinars, and seminars.

You may assist others succeed by encouraging them and encouraging ongoing progress. Encouragement fosters confidence and self-belief, while continuous improvement establishes quantifiable targets and keeps individuals on track with their aims. Both are necessary for success and may be the difference between failure and success.

*Encouragement And Overall Success

When it comes to achieving success, encouragement is an important factor. Encouragement is a form of positive reinforcement that can help motivate and inspire people to reach their goals. It can also be a way of showing appreciation for all the hard work someone has put in.

Encouragement is not just about praising someone for their efforts but rather providing support, feedback, and direction to help them reach their desired outcomes. A key element of encouragement is understanding the individual's strengths and weaknesses and tailoring advice to best suit them.

Encouragement can come in many forms, including verbal compliments, written notes, special rewards, or simply offering a listening ear. With encouragement, people are more likely to have the confidence and motivation to persist in difficult situations and stay on track with their goals.

It's also important to remember that success doesn't always come easily. It often requires dedication, determination, and hard work. That's why having a supportive network of family, friends, colleagues, or mentors is essential for overall success.

Having a strong support system will provide individuals with both emotional and practical resources to help them reach their goals. This can include giving advice and guidance, providing moral support, helping out with tasks or errands, or just being there to listen.

Overall, encouragement is an important tool for helping individuals achieve success. By providing moral support and practical assistance, people are more likely to feel motivated and driven to reach their goals. With a combination of determination and encouragement, anything is possible

CHAPTER 7

*Success Encouragement at home

Parents play an important role in helping their children achieve success. By providing children with encouragement and support, parents can help boost their children's self-confidence, foster a positive attitude towards learning, and motivate them to reach their goals.

Encouragement is a powerful tool for helping children reach their full potential. Here are some tips for how to encourage your child at home:

1. **Demonstrate your belief in them** – A child's confidence can be damaged when a parent shows a lack of faith in their abilities. Show your child that you believe in them by complimenting them on their achievements, applauding their efforts, and expressing your pride in their successes.

2. **Promote a growth mindset** – Encourage your child to view challenges as learning opportunities and to persist in the face of failure. Teach your child that mistakes are part of the learning process and mistakes can be used as stepping stones to success.

3. **Provide structure and guidance** – Make sure your child understands what is expected of them and give them the guidance they need to succeed. Establish a set of rules and consequences to ensure your child stays on track with their school work and other activities.

4. **Set realistic goals** – Set age-appropriate goals and expectations for your child. Make sure your expectations are realistic and achievable so your child can feel successful when they reach those goals.

5. **Celebrate successes** – Recognize and celebrate your child's accomplishments, no matter how small they may be. Let your child know that you are proud of them and their successes.

By taking the time to provide encouragement, structure, and guidance, you can help set your child up for success both now and in the future.

*How can you Encourage Yourself

1. **Set goals** – Setting goals for yourself is a great way to stay motivated and inspired. When you have a goal in mind, it gives you something to work towards and keeps you focused on your progress.

Make sure the goals you set are achievable, measurable, and time-bound.

2. **Celebrate achievements** – No matter how small, celebrate every success along the way. This will help you keep your motivation and remind you that even if you are making small steps, they are steps forward nonetheless.

3. **Take care of yourself** – Don't forget to look after yourself physically, mentally and emotionally. Whether that means taking time out for yourself, eating healthy meals, exercising or just having a few moments of 'me' time; make sure you do something for yourself everyday that helps you relax and destress.

4. **Stay positive** – Focus on the positive aspects of your life. Remind yourself of all the things you've achieved and be grateful for what you have. Choose to stay away from negative people and situations and surround yourself with those who encourage you and lift you up.

5. **Change your environment** – Your environment can have a big impact on how motivated and inspired you feel. Take some time to change up your surroundings or find ways to make it more inspiring and motivating. This could be anything from getting new items of clothing that make you feel good to brightening up your workspace with vibrant colors.

6. **Talk to someone** – If you feel like nothing is working, it can be helpful to talk to someone about it. Talking to a friend or family member can help you gain clarity and perspective on the situation, as well as provide support when you need it.

^x What are examples of Encouraging Words

Encouraging words can help to build self-esteem, motivate others and inspire greatness. Some examples of encouraging words include:

• You are capable.
• You are strong.
• You have the power to succeed.
• Believe in yourself.
• Anything is possible.

- I believe in you.
- You can do it.
- You have what it takes.
- You are special.
- Never give up.
- Keep trying.
- Follow your dreams.
- Take one step at a time.
- You are worth it.
- Have faith in yourself.
- Everything will be alright.

*What is the Best Motivation for Success

Success can come from a variety of sources, but often the most powerful type of motivation is encouragement. Encouragement is not simply positive words or affirmations – it's about believing in someone and providing the support necessary for them to reach their goals. Encouragement also includes providing constructive feedback to help the individual understand their strengths and weaknesses so they can become more successful.

Encouragement helps individuals push themselves and keep going, even when things get difficult or challenging. When individuals receive encouragement, it reinforces their desire to succeed, builds self-esteem and confidence, and motivates them to persist and strive even further.

Encouragement doesn't have to be limited to spoken words; it can also include physical actions such as providing resources and opportunities to learn, introducing new experiences, and showing support in other ways. Even simple gestures like a pat on the back or a hug can go a long way towards inspiring success.

Ultimately, success is achieved through hard work, dedication, and resilience. But having a supportive network of people who truly believe in you can be just as important. Encouragement serves as a reminder that someone has your back and will be there to cheer you on along your journey. That can make all the difference in achieving success.

* What is a Good Sentence for Encouragement

"You have the power and ability to achieve great success - all you need to do is believe in yourself and never give up!"

* What are 5 synonyms for Encouragement

1. **Inspiration** – Motivating others to strive for their goals and better themselves.
2. **Motivation** – Encouraging someone to take action towards their goals.
3. **Support** – Offering emotional and physical aid to help another achieve success.
4. **Boost** – Giving someone an extra push to reach their goals.
5. **Upliftment** – Helping someone to stay positive and reach their dreams.

Encouragement is one of the most powerful tools we can use to help others succeed. It can be a way to remind someone of their worth, give them hope, or just be there when they need it most. By providing support and boosting morale, we can foster a sense of confidence and determination in others. And when we offer words of encouragement, we provide motivation that can drive people to success. Synonyms for encouragement can help us express our thoughts and feelings in more detail, allowing us to create an even more impactful message.

No matter how small the act may be, using words of encouragement to inspire and motivate others can have a lasting effect. So next time you want to lift someone up, don't be afraid to use synonyms for encouragement like inspiration, motivation, support, boost, and upliftment!

*What are the 7 Types of Motivation

1. **Intrinsic motivation**: This sort of motivation arises from inside a person and is motivated by the joy or pleasure one experiences while attaining a goal. It is motivated by personal curiosity, delight, and enthusiasm and does not need external incentives or accolades.
2. **Extrinsic motivation:** This sort of motivation originates from outside of a person and may be beneficial or bad. Praise, awards, and incentives are examples of positive extrinsic motivation. Punishments, deadlines, and other types of coercion are examples of negative forms of extrinsic motivation.

3. **Goal-oriented motivation**: This happens when a person is driven to finish a task or attain a goal. It entails defining attainable goals and taking efforts to achieve them with the purpose of reaching a desired result.

4. **Achievement motivation**: This drive is striving for achievement and recognition. It is motivated by the desire to achieve, to outperform others, and to be proud of one's accomplishments.

5. **Social motivation**: The need to belong and be accepted by others is referred to as social motivation. Building connections, obtaining approval and acceptance, and being loved by others are all part of it.

6. **Fear motivation**: When a person is driven by the fear of failure or punishment, this is referred to as fear-based motivation. It is often used to compel someone into doing something they would not otherwise do.

7. Curiosity-driven motivation: This sort of motivation stems from a desire to learn about new ideas, thoughts, and experiences. It entails obtaining information and participating in activities that broaden one's knowledge and understanding.

Understanding the many levels of motivation may assist people in determining what drives them the most and why they are compelled to accomplish particular things. Individuals may utilize these distinct sorts of motivation to establish methods for attaining their objectives and creating good changes in their life if they understand them.

*<u>What is a Daily Encouragement</u>

A daily encouragement is any type of positive support or motivation that can help you achieve success. It may come in the form of words of affirmation, inspiring quotes, or even kind gestures. The idea is to help people stay motivated and on track with their goals. This type of encouragement can be incredibly powerful in helping people succeed.

Studies have shown that having positive reinforcement from outside sources can significantly increase an individual's chances of achieving success. Encouragement from friends and family can help build confidence and self-esteem, and this can lead to better performance in school, work, and other areas of life. It's also important to remember that it's not just about receiving external support; it's also about giving it. Showing others that you believe in them and their potential can go a long way towards building trust and inspiring them to reach for their goals.

There are several ways to provide daily encouragement, such as leaving uplifting messages around the house, sending encouraging texts, or simply sharing your successes with someone who needs a boost. No matter how small the gesture, it can make a big difference when it comes to motivating someone to succeed.

At the end of the day, providing daily encouragement is a powerful way to build trust, motivate others, and ultimately help create a more positive environment for everyone involved. So the next time you're feeling discouraged or overwhelmed by life's challenges, remember that there is always someone out there willing to give you the support you need to keep going and achieve success!

*Why is Encouragement Important in School

Encouragement is a powerful tool that may be utilized to help pupils thrive in the classroom. According to research, when students get positive feedback and encouragement from their professors, they are more likely to be motivated and put forth effort. Students are more likely to remain involved and focused on the subject at hand when they feel acknowledged and encouraged.

Encouragement also improves pupils' self-esteem and confidence. When students are praised for their hard work and efforts, they begin to trust in themselves more and are willing to take chances in order to achieve their objectives. Furthermore, encouraging remarks from their instructor may push pupils to go harder and go above their expectations.

Furthermore, encouraging students and instructors in the classroom helps foster a feeling of trust. When instructors make an effort to acknowledge each student's unique skills and flaws, they may build an accepting atmosphere. This not only makes pupils feel appreciated, but it also encourages them to be more receptive to comments and accept constructive criticism.

Finally, encouragement at school is crucial since it contributes to a pleasant environment. Students are more willing to share ideas, be creative, and have fun in the classroom when they feel acknowledged and encouraged by their instructor. This may result in a better overall learning experience.

Finally, encouragement is a crucial tool that may be utilized in the classroom to assist students attain their full potential and to foster a bond between teacher and student. Encouragement from a teacher may assist promote a respectful environment, create a pleasant mood, and motivate pupils to strive for success.

*What are 2 Words for Encourage

The words encouragement and support are often used to describe the act of encouraging someone. Encouragement is the act of giving someone emotional support, acceptance, or guidance in order to inspire them to accomplish their objectives or to assist them in times of difficulty. Support is when you provide someone assistance or resources to help them reach their objectives. Both phrases describe methods of encouraging others, albeit at varying degrees of intensity. Encouragement is more broad and supportive, while support is more particular and direct.

*Why is Encouragement Important for a Child

Encouragement is essential in assisting youngsters in reaching their full potential. It is critical to encourage children so that they may develop self-confidence, resilience, and a feeling of purpose and success.

Children are motivated and confident when they are encouraged. When children get positive feedback from adults, they are more likely to stick with their objectives and overcome obstacles. A supportive atmosphere that encourages the formation of good attitudes and beliefs may aid in their success.

Encouragement also assists youngsters in developing positive connections with others. Encouragement via words and conduct may help youngsters feel more at ease in social circumstances and open to connecting with others. This may result in enhanced self-esteem, communication skills, and social functioning.

Finally, encouragement aids in the development of intrinsic drive to study in youngsters. Children are more inclined to pursue their hobbies and learn new skills when they feel encouraged and welcomed. It may also help kids develop a feeling of independence and responsibility.

To summarize, encouragement is critical for assisting youngsters in reaching their greatest potential. Parents, teachers, and other adults may provide children with the skills they need to lead successful lives by creating a supportive and encouraging atmosphere.

CHAPTER 8

*How can we Encourage Others in their Hard Times

It may be quite tough for someone to go through a difficult or unpleasant period in their life. Whether it's a medical sickness, an emotional condition, or just feeling overwhelmed by life's demands, we all need a little extra encouragement and support from time to time. That is why it is important to reach out and provide words of encouragement and support to people who are hurting.

Even though it seems to be a little gesture, encouraging someone may have a significant influence on them. It may make children feel supported and powerful in the face of whatever difficulties they may be experiencing. Here are some ways you may inspire someone:

1. **Listen to them**: Simply listening to someone without passing judgment is one of the most impactful things you can do. Allow them to discuss and vent, then support their sentiments by expressing your understanding. This might give them a sense of being heard and understood, which can be really powerful.

2. **Provide assistance**: Another method to show your support is to offer assistance, even if it is as simple as running an errand or cooking supper for them. Offering aid demonstrates that you are concerned about their well-being and want to assist them in any way you can.

3. **Send positive messages**: Another fantastic approach to show someone you care is to text or write good, uplifting notes. It conveys to them that you are thinking about them and wishing them well at this trying time.

4. **Find common ground**: Recognizing someone's unique circumstances and hardships is vital, but finding a connecting point between you and the individual may also be quite beneficial. Sharing a humorous anecdote, referring to a similar event, or providing advise based on your own life experiences may all bring comfort and support in their present position.

In stressful circumstances, a few simple words of encouragement may make a significant difference in someone's mental health and wellness. Take the opportunity to reach out and give your assistance to others who may need it.

*How do you Respond to Encouragement

In order to succeed, it is imperative to surround yourself with positivity. That positivity may come in many forms including, but not limited to, encouragement from friends and family, advice from mentors, and support from the masses. No matter who we are, we can all benefit from a word of encouragement now and then. That is to say, how do you respond when someone compliments you? The first step is to understand that encouragement is a positive force. It might be in the form of supportive words or a gentle touch on the back. Regardless of the source, it's vital that you recognize that someone took the time to commend your hard work. Taking encouragement to heart and accepting that you are being encouraged are two keys to moving forward and achieving your success. It's a sign that someone believes in you and has faith in your abilities. While you take words of encouragement to heart, it's important to take action as well. For instance, when someone compliments your work ethic, you should use that to encourage you to work even harder. When somebody congratulates you on your success, turn it into a chance to set new goals and keep trying. Furthermore, don't forget to thank those who have offered their encouragement. A short, simple thank you will help encourage them. Having these sorts of positive relationships also makes it easier for you to make connections and stay up to date on one another's progress. The encouragement of others is essential for achieving one's goals and it's an important step in the journey that should not be shied away from. Encouragement is your friend.

*What is the Meaning of Encouragingly

Encouragingly is the activity of encouraging or inspiring someone to achieve their objectives or to persevere in the face of adversity. It is a kind of positive reinforcement that may assist individuals in developing and realizing their full potential. Encouragement is giving someone encouragement, support, direction, and inspiration to help them find the confidence and drive they need to achieve their objectives.

Words of praise, admiration, and compliments, as well as specific advise and direction, may all be kinds of encouragement. It may also involve physical benefits such as gratitude tokens or awards. It is critical to understand that encouragement is not the same as manipulation or compulsion; it should originate from a genuine concern for the individual's advancement and development. Encouragement, when done appropriately, may be a tremendous instrument for personal growth and development. It may help people understand their own potential, gain confidence in themselves, and form meaningful connections with others. Furthermore, it may be good to society as a whole: by cultivating a culture of mutual support and respect, we can build a better world for everybody.

*What does it Mean to Encourage Someone

Encouragement is methods of giving someone with positive reinforcement in order to assist them achieve their objectives. Encouragement may take numerous forms, ranging from verbal praise and praises to physical acts such as a hug or slap on the back. Encouragement, in whatever form, is about offering support, increasing self-confidence, and assisting the individual in realizing that they can achieve their objectives and be successful. Encouragement may also be considered an act of kindness since it aids in the development of relationships and the creation of a supportive atmosphere. When someone supports another person, they demonstrate that they care about that person's well-being and success. This form of assistance may make a significant impact in someone's life and assist them in reaching their objectives.

Telling someone you believe in them or that you are proud of their efforts might be enough to encourage them. It may also be more concrete, such as providing practical guidance or assistance with chores relevant to their goal's achievement. Encouragement, in whatever shape it takes, is a crucial aspect in assisting others to thrive and fulfill their full potential.

*Is Encouragement the Same as Support

Depending on the circumstances, the answer to this question might be both yes and no. Encouragement is a kind of support, but it is much more than that. Encouragement entails offering additional incentive, acknowledgment, or positive reinforcement to assist someone achieve a goal.

Encouragement may take many forms. It may be a word of encouragement, a tap on the back, or a word of affirmation. It might also take the shape of material presents or exceptional privileges. It is vital to remember that encouragement should not be mistaken with praise. When you praise someone, you are telling them they are doing well; when you encourage them, you are telling them they can do even better.

Support, on the other hand, focuses on giving emotional and practical assistance. This might include providing resources, guidance, or just being there for someone in need. Support is often seen as more realistic and less emotional than encouragement.

So, to answer the question, is encouragement the same as support? The answer is no. Encouragement is a kind of support, but it is also much more. It is an act of offering extra incentive and acknowledgment that may assist someone in reaching their objectives. At the same time, support gives emotional and practical assistance that is not always tied to achieving objectives. Both types of aid may be critical in assisting someone to achieve, therefore it's critical to identify and use both.

* <u>What is Something that Encourages a person to do Something</u>

When it comes to obtaining achievement, encouragement is the single most significant aspect. It is critical to establish a supportive atmosphere in order to motivate someone and assist them in reaching their objectives. Encouragement may be the difference between success and failure for an individual or a team. Verbal affirmations, physical prizes, goal setting, and constructive criticism are all types of encouragement.

One of the most powerful types of encouragement is verbal affirmation. People want validation and appreciation in order to remain motivated and believe in themselves. Hearing someone say "you're doing a fantastic job" or "I believe in you" might be enough to motivate someone to reach their objectives.

Another powerful kind of incentive is monetary prizes. People tend to react favorably when they are recognized for their work, whether it is a modest gift, a certificate of success, or a raise. It allows individuals to see that their efforts are paying off and provides them with something practical to aspire towards.

Setting goals is an essential technique for motivating people to realize their maximum potential. It helps to define expectations, motivates people, and sets a schedule for when particular goals should be completed. It also offers them something to aim for and strive for.

Another kind of encouragement that may be used to assist someone improve their performance is constructive criticism. It is critical to offer constructive criticism that is aimed at improving rather than punishing. This form of feedback assists individuals in identifying areas where they may develop and provides them with the tools to do so.

Encouragement is a critical component of success. It may take many different forms, such as vocal affirmations, physical prizes, goal setting, and constructive criticism. Creating a supportive atmosphere is critical for assisting people and teams in reaching their greatest potential.

*How Does Encouragement Improve Performance

Encouragement can have a profound impact on performance, both in the short and long term. Encouragement is an act of support, validation, and affirmation that can give people the strength and courage to take risks and accomplish goals they otherwise may not attempt.

When someone receives positive words from others, it gives them a feeling of being accepted and valued which helps to boost their self-confidence and self-esteem. This in turn gives them the drive and motivation to work harder, longer and more efficiently to achieve success. It also reduces fear of failure and encourages risk-taking, which can lead to greater accomplishments.

Furthermore, encouragement helps to increase morale in the workplace. When employees feel supported by their peers and management, they are more likely to take initiative and complete tasks with excellence. When employees know that their efforts will be rewarded with recognition, it encourages them to continue striving for excellence.

Encouragement also reinforces good behavior in the workplace. When people receive positive reinforcement for their actions, they are more likely to keep up those behaviors rather than engaging in activities that could be detrimental to their careers or organizations. This can help create a culture of teamwork and collaboration that encourages growth and achievement.

Finally, encouraging words can help people build strong relationships. When people are encouraged by others, they often want to reciprocate that same positivity with those around them, creating a stronger sense of trust and loyalty between coworkers, family members, and friends.

Encouragement is invaluable tools in helping people reach their full potential. By giving people praise for their efforts and helping them remain confident, motivated and inspired, you can help them reach greater heights of success.

*Is Encouragement an Attitude

Yes, there is a resounding yes to this question. Encouragement is an attitude as well as a significant success instrument. It is a method of recognizing potential, motivating people, and providing a supporting atmosphere to assist them in reaching their objectives. Encouragement has the ability to inspire and drive individuals to act. Someone who is encouraged is more inclined to be productive and to take chances. They will gain confidence and become more self-sufficient. Encouragement may also boost one's self-esteem and make them feel more respected and loved.

Encouragement is useful not just to the receiver but also to those who provide it. Encouragement may enhance morale and build a pleasant work atmosphere. It also shows respect, trust, and gratitude for the individual's efforts.

Encouragement is a necessary component of every successful team or organization. It fosters connections, improves communication, and promotes growth and development. Encouraged people are more likely to be engaged and driven. They will be more productive and have a stronger feeling of purpose.

In conclusion, it is apparent that encouragement is an attitude that may make or break a person's ability to attain their full potential and accomplish success. It may provide people the encouragement and inspiration they need to achieve their objectives and make a difference in their life. Encouraging others is a long-term investment that fosters great connections and improves team performance.

* **What Happens when you Encourage**

Encouragement will raise confidence, increase motivation and productivity, and make individuals feel appreciated. Encouraging others may help them accomplish their objectives, become better versions of themselves, and discover hidden potential.

When we offer someone encouragement, it might give them the confidence to attempt something new or take on a challenge. It may also aid in the development of trust, the strengthening of friendships, and the promotion of good cooperation. Furthermore, encouraging others shows them that we believe in them and are there to assist them.

Encouragement encourages people to accept responsibility for their own accomplishments and mistakes, which may lead to self-empowerment and a feeling of self-efficacy. When we encourage others and remind them of their accomplishments, they experience a feeling of pride and achievement.

Offering encouragement is fundamentally about recognizing and appreciating the qualities and efforts of others. It instills in individuals the feeling that they are capable of great things. We can assist people realize their greatest potential by expressing encouragement.

***How do you use Encouraged**

Encouragement is one of the most important tools you can use in order to help people reach success. Encouragement helps motivate and inspire people to strive for their goals and to not give up. It's important to be mindful of how you use encouragement and know when it's necessary. Here are some tips on how to use encouragement effectively:

1. **Create a positive environment** – Creating an environment that is supportive and encouraging will help foster motivation and enthusiasm for achieving success.
2. **Praise people for their efforts** – Praise individuals for the effort they have put into something, even if it doesn't turn out as planned.
3. **Lead by example** – Show your team or group what it takes to succeed by setting a positive example.
4. **Give meaningful feedback** – Provide constructive feedback that helps people develop their skills and reach success.
5. **Celebrate successes** – Acknowledge accomplishments, big or small, to keep people motivated and encouraged.

By following these steps and using encouragement effectively, you can help others reach success. It's important to remember that everyone responds differently to different forms of encouragement, so it's important to be mindful of what works best for each person you are working with. Encouragement should always be used with kindness and respect, as well as in conjunction with other effective strategies like goal setting and hard work.

*<u>What are the Components of</u> <u>Encouragement</u>

Encouragement is an important factor in achieving success. It can be defined as words, actions, and environment that help people to believe in themselves and gain confidence in their abilities. Encouragement can be a powerful tool to help people strive for excellence and reach their goals.

The components of encouragement are:

1. **Validation**: Showing someone that their efforts and achievements are noticed and appreciated. Positive feedback from peers, family, and friends can motivate people to keep pushing forward.
2. **Support**: Giving someone the tools, resources, and advice they need to succeed. This could be physical resources, such as providing them with the necessary materials for their project, or emotional

support, such as offering words of encouragement or being there to listen when they need it.

3. **Trust**: Believing in someone's potential even when they don't yet have the confidence or experience to do so themselves. This can come in the form of offering challenges or tasks to complete, with the belief that they will rise to the occasion.

4. **Opportunity**: Providing chances for someone to learn new skills or take on additional responsibilities. This can include giving them additional assignments, introducing them to a mentor or other leaders in the field, or offering training courses.

Encouragement is an essential part of achieving success, and it's important to remember that everyone responds differently to different types of encouragement. Tailoring encouragement to an individual's needs and interests can make a big difference in their ability to achieve success

CHAPTER 9

*What is an Example of Encouragement

Encouragement is the act of encouraging and motivating someone to achieve their objectives. It may range from simple words of encouragement to more complex gestures such as actual incentives. Encouragement is the act of encouraging someone to act, better themselves, and achieve success.

A parent assuring their kid that they believe in them and will always support them is an example of encouragement. Another example is a teacher informing a pupil that they are capable of success and that they have what it takes to achieve great things. A third example is a buddy telling another friend that they can accomplish everything they put their minds to and that they would always be there for them. All of these are instances of how encouragement may help someone achieve and succeed in their objectives.

* What is Encouragement Motivation

Encouragement motivation is the process of inspiring and motivating someone to achieve their objectives by utilizing positive reinforcement. It entails acknowledging an individual's qualities and triumphs, encouraging them, and assisting them in focusing on the positives. Encouragement is critical to an individual's success because it provides them the confidence and motivation to keep trying even when things seem challenging. Friends, relatives, mentors, coaches, and even strangers may provide encouragement. When it comes to encouraging, keep in mind that everyone has various motives and needs, therefore it is critical to figure out what connects with each person in order to deliver effective encouragement. Some individuals, for example, may react better to positive reinforcement than others to constructive criticism or instruction. It is critical to be aware of the individual's requirements and to customize your support appropriately.

Verbal praise, physical gestures, and material incentives are all types of encouragement. When utilized effectively, encouragement may help a person remain motivated and work towards their objectives. Encouragement, in addition to giving inspiration and support, aids in the development of connections and the creation of a feeling of belonging. People are more likely to get involved in their own achievement and believe in themselves if they are provided with a secure and supportive atmosphere in which to achieve their objectives.

Finally, supporting someone to achieve their objectives is about establishing confidence in them and demonstrating to them that they are capable of accomplishment. Anyone, with the appropriate amount of encouragement and determination, can make their aspirations a reality.

*Who is your Greatest Source of Encouragement

The greatest source of encouragement in life is often your closest loved ones. Friends, family, and mentors can provide essential support, guidance, and motivation to help you achieve success. When you are feeling overwhelmed or discouraged, they are often the first people to step in with words of encouragement that can help you push through and reach your goals.

Your friends and family have known you for a long time and understand what drives you to succeed. They may remind you of past successes to bolster your confidence and reassure you of your ability to handle difficult tasks. They may also be willing to lend a hand if needed to help you complete challenging tasks.

Mentors can also provide invaluable encouragement, especially when it comes to goal setting and reaching your ambitions. They bring knowledge and experience from their own success stories, as well as a network of contacts that can open new doors for you. From suggesting new ideas to offering critiques, mentors can help you stay focused and motivated on reaching your objectives.

No matter who you turn to for encouragement, having someone who believes in you can make all the difference. Knowing that you have the support of those who care about you can give you the strength and determination to face any challenge and succeed.

*Why Encouragement is Important in Learning and Development

Encouragement has an important role in the learning and development process. It gives people a feeling of purpose and keeps them motivated and involved in the learning process. It may also assist to boost confidence and foster an atmosphere in which students feel safe taking chances and pushing themselves to reach their objectives.

Encouragement contributes to the creation of a constructive environment in which students are encouraged to think critically and solve issues on their own. It encourages students to take charge of their own learning and accept responsibility for their triumphs and failings. Encouragement and positive reinforcement may help learners stay interested, focused, and motivated.

Encouragement also aids in the development of connections between students and teachers. It is much simpler for instructors and students to work together and cooperate on projects when they have a relationship founded on trust, respect, and understanding.

With support, students feel secure taking chances and sharing ideas without fear of being judged or failing.

Encouragement also creates a feeling of security, enabling students to experiment with new ideas without fear of failure or shame. Positive feedback from professors helps students see the importance of their effort, especially when they are suffering. Encouragement offers students the confidence they need to persevere through challenges and emerge stronger in the end.

Finally, encouragement is vital in learning and development because it helps learners establish a feeling of community. A supportive workplace promotes peer cooperation and communication, which may lead to more meaningful and effective learning experiences. Finally, encouragement is an essential component of the learning and growth process. It contributes to the creation of a good environment that fosters risk-taking and independence, as well as the development of connections between instructors and pupils. Encouragement also gives learners a feeling of comfort and self-confidence, allowing them to persevere through challenges and emerge stronger in the end.

* <u>What Encouragement Does God give us</u>

God's Word is a wonderful source of encouragement. It is filled with promises, reminders of His love, and encouragement for the future. "May the God of hope fill you with all joy and peace as you trust in Him, so that you may overflow with hope by the power of the Holy Spirit," Paul says in Romans 15:5. This passage reminds us that God wants to fill us with pleasure and serenity, and it encourages us to put our confidence in Him to do so.

"This is the day that the Lord has created; let us rejoice and be happy in it," reads Psalm 118:24. This passage reminds us to be appreciative for each day, regardless of what occurs. We may rejoice in the fact that every day is a gift from God.

Psalm 27:14 is also a significant source of inspiration for us. "Wait for the Lord; be strong and take heart, and wait for the Lord," it says. This passage urges us to continue to trust God even when circumstances seem challenging. He will never abandon us and will always be there to assist us in our times of need.

Finally, Isaiah 40:31 urges us to persevere even when we want to give up. "But those who trust in the Lord will replenish their strength," it says. They will fly like eagles, run without being tired, and walk without becoming weak." This passage reminds us that God provides us with strength and urges us to go on regardless of our circumstances.

God's Word is a great source of hope. We might be reminded of His affection for us and His future promises when we read it. We may be inspired to remain firm in our faith, to be grateful for each day, and to persevere even when circumstances seem tough. God is constantly there to provide us the encouragement and support we need to face life's obstacles.

*What is Personal Encouragement

Personal encouragement is the act of giving someone support and praise, usually via words or actions. It is a technique to show someone that you believe in them and that they have the potential to achieve. It may take numerous forms, including praises, good comments, and expressions of thanks. Encouragement also entails listening with an open mind and heart, offering useful advise and recommendations, and recognizing accomplishments.

Encouragement may be utilized in various parts of life, from education to job to personal relationships. It is particularly beneficial when a person is confronting a tough situation or is feeling disheartened. A few words of encouragement may go a long way toward helping someone remain motivated and achieve achievement.

The effectiveness of personal encouragement rests in its capacity to improve self-esteem and confidence while also providing someone with the bravery and fortitude needed to face problems.

Encouragement helps individuals feel valued and respected, which may improve their general perspective and mood. Encouragement may help someone accomplish higher heights and realize their objectives by offering a feeling of stability and support.

*How Do you Write a Note of Encouragement

Writing a note of encouragement will be a really important way to show someone you care. It may be used to convey gratitude, to remind someone of their value, and to remind them that they are capable of great things.

Consider the following suggestions while writing a message of encouragement:

1. **Begin with an encouraging phrase**: Begin by explaining why you're writing and why you believe in them. Whether it's a thank you for their hard work or an acknowledgement of a goal they've attained, start with something that will brighten their spirits.

2. **Give specific compliments**: Your message should not be loaded with generic praises, but rather should highlight unique characteristics or achievements that have struck out to you. This will assist the receiver in understanding why they are being appreciated and recognizing the effect of their efforts.

3. **Provide assistance and advice**: If the receiver is having difficulty with anything, volunteer to help or give advice as required. Knowing that someone believes in them and wants to assist them may be very comforting and inspiring.

4. **Close Positively**: End your message by wishing the receiver well in their efforts and expressing your confidence in their capacity to achieve.

A note of encouragement is a strong gesture that may have a long-term influence on someone. It might help them remain motivated and recall why they should keep working towards their objectives. Use these suggestions to send an encouraging and uplifting message that will remind them of their worth and importance!

*Overcoming Obstacles through Encouragement

We all experience obstacles in our life, some bigger than others. It may be very tough to persevere in the face of hardship, but there are methods to make the road more bearable. Encouragement is one of the most powerful ways to help oneself achieve. When someone provides you support, guidance, or a kind word in order to assist you achieve your objectives, this is referred to as encouragement.

It is critical to remember that encouraging others is just as vital as being encouraged. It is very fulfilling and useful for everyone concerned when you are able to supply others with the inspiration they need to attain success.

Encouragement may come from a variety of people, including family, friends, instructors, mentors, and even strangers. Knowing that someone has your back and believes in you may be quite empowering. This may help you stay focused on your objective while also giving you the confidence to take chances and push yourself. Another excellent source of motivation is to read inspiring tales or comments from individuals who have previously achieved achievement. Reading the tales of others who have overcome comparable challenges might give you hope that you, too, can achieve. Furthermore, there are several free internet sites that provide words of wisdom from successful people that you may utilize as motivation through tough times.

Finally, keep in mind that sometimes the finest source of encouragement comes from inside. Learning to trust your intuition and believing in yourself may be tremendous tools for success. Whether it's attaining a professional milestone, mastering a skill, or overcoming an obstacle, self-confidence may be critical to realizing your full potential.

Encouragement is important in life because it may help us continue ahead even when things seem insurmountable. Taking use of family and friend support, as well as searching out inspiring tales and quotations, are excellent strategies to remain motivated and achieve your objectives. Nothing is impossible with the proper mindset and a little drive!

*How do you Stay Encouraged by God

It might be tough to keep motivated and find the strength to go ahead when you are feeling down and frustrated. There are, however, other sources of strength and encouragement accessible to us, including trust in God.

God has given us the ability and strength to conquer every challenge. Every day, He encourages us via His Word, reminding us of His constancy, love, and provision. We may also remain encouraged by spending time with Him in prayer and reading the Bible on a regular basis. We may share Him our troubles and fears in prayer, knowing that He is our source of strength. Reading the Bible may help us stay focused on God's intentions for us and refresh our confidence in Him.

Another method to remain encouraged by God is to seek direction and encouragement from other Christians. God has asked us to love one another and to assist one another in times of need. We may share our troubles and pains with one another and find hope and encouragement through building meaningful connections with other Christians.

Finally, even though we may feel disheartened at times, God has not given up on us. He is with us every step of the journey, bestowing love and compassion on us. We may have hope in Him because He will provide for our needs and work all things together for good. Remember that no matter how difficult life seems at times, God is always there to bring encouragement and strength. He never fails and is always loyal. Seek Him out today and trust Him to see you through whatever comes your way.

*What are the Two Ways of Encouragement

Encouragement is a powerful tool that may help us accomplish our objectives and fulfill our aspirations. It may give the drive and inspiration required to continue ahead. There are two kinds of encouragement: external and internal.

External encouragement is when someone from outside of ourselves supports us. It might take the shape of praises or compliments, words of encouragement, physical prizes, public acknowledgment, or any other type of positive reinforcement. This form of encouragement helps us believe in ourselves and gives us the strength to act.

Internal encouragement is when we encourage oneself. We may achieve this by compiling a list of our successes, rewarding ourselves for attaining objectives, taking time to rest and recharge, concentrating on positive thinking, and creating a pleasant atmosphere for ourselves. This kind of support helps us keep focused and motivated, as well as on track with our objectives. Encouragement, in whatever form it appears, is an essential component of attaining success. Both external and internal motivation may help us achieve our objectives and live up to our full potential. We may give ourselves the push we need to succeed by applying both sorts of encouragement.

CHAPTER 10

*What are the 5 Main Factors which can Lead to Success of a Person?

1. **Dedication**: Dedication is the key to success and an important factor that can lead to achieving one's goals and objectives. It requires a person to devote his/her time and effort to reach the desired outcome.

2. **Hard work**: Hard work is essential for success and it involves taking initiative, being persistent, and having a strong work ethic.

Working hard and smart will allow a person to become successful in the long run.

3. **Goal setting**: Setting and working towards realistic goals is an essential part of success. Goals provide direction and structure to the plans you make, helping you stay focused and motivated on the path to success.

4. **Self-belief**: Having self-belief is crucial for success as it enables a person to push through obstacles and difficult times with confidence. Believing in oneself can help overcome any doubts or fears that may arise.

5. **Encouragement:** Last but not least, encouragement plays a major role in achieving success. It serves as a reminder that we can do anything we put our minds to, regardless of the challenge. Receiving support from those around us can be inspiring and help us reach our full potential.

*What are the Keys of Success?

We all want to be successful, yet it may seem like an unattainable goal at times. Fortunately, there are some keys that may assist us in achieving success in our life. Encouragement is one of the most crucial keys. Encouragement gives us a feeling of drive and inspiration, which may help us achieve our objectives.

The act of delivering positive reinforcement to someone or something is known as encouragement. This might be vocal praise, assistance, or just acknowledging their efforts. It motivates us to persevere even when things seem tough or disheartening. Encouragement may come from family, friends, mentors, coworkers, and even people with no direct relationship to us. Encouragement gives us the desire and confidence we need to push ourselves to achieve our objectives. Positive reinforcement and appreciation of our efforts encourages us to keep trying for achievement, even when it seems unattainable or frightening. Furthermore, encouragement may give much-needed mental and emotional support as we strive toward our objectives.

It is important to realize that success does not occur overnight. It needs perseverance and commitment. Having support along the road may make or break our ability to achieve our objectives and aspirations. Encouragement keeps us motivated and on track toward our ultimate objective. Building a supporting network of individuals who will provide words of encouragement and support during our journey is critical.

Encouragement is a crucial asset for anybody seeking success in any aspect of life. It gives us the inspiration, confidence, and support we need to keep going even when things are difficult. We can go one step closer to our objectives with a strong network of supporters delivering words of encouragement and acknowledgment.

*What are the Steps to Success?

We all want to be successful, but it doesn't come easily. It takes devotion and hard effort, as well as a strong feeling of self-confidence and belief in one's capacity to achieve any objective. Although success means various things to different individuals, there are several fundamental actions that everybody can take to improve their chances of reaching their goals.

Making a plan is the first step toward success. A plan gives you direction and purpose in accomplishing your objectives. It is simpler to keep on track and guarantee that you are taking the essential actions to attain your intended goal if you outline what needs to be done.

The next stage is to cultivate a good attitude and mindset. It is critical to have a good attitude in order to make progress toward achievement. It is also critical to have reasonable expectations and a strong feeling of self-belief. Maintaining a positive attitude can help you remain motivated and more likely to accomplish your objectives.

Having a support system is the third stage to success. It is critical to surround oneself with individuals who believe in your goal and can give support along the road. Friends and family members may be a tremendous source of motivation as well as assist you keep yourself responsible for your activities. Mentors or coaches may also provide helpful guidance and insights on how to achieve your objectives.

Taking action is the fourth phase. Setting attainable goals and really completing the required effort to come closer to your goal are examples of this. When it comes to obtaining success, taking chances may be helpful and sometimes required, but it's crucial to have a backup plan in case things don't go as planned.

Finally, the fifth key to success is to retain a good attitude in the face of adversity. Everyone has difficulties along the route, but it is important to keep going no matter what. By being motivated and maintaining a positive attitude, you are more likely to overcome any hurdles and finally arrive at your target.

Finally, there are some crucial actions that one may do to improve their chances of success. Creating a strategy, keeping a good attitude, having a support system, taking action, and being determined are all necessary stages on the path to success. Anyone may achieve their goals with hard effort, commitment, and support.

*How Encouragement is the Key to Success

Encouragement is the key to success in every industry or area of life. It has been shown that when individuals are encouraged, they work harder and longer than those who are not. When individuals feel recognized and encouraged, they are more likely to set greater objectives, work hard to accomplish them, and succeed. Encouragement inspires people to put out effort and work hard in order to achieve. A strong sense of purpose may have a profound influence on people and help them overcome obstacles.

Furthermore, feeling encouraged may give a person the confidence to take chances, which can frequently lead to favorable outcomes and bigger accomplishments. Taking measured risks may lead to more innovative ideas and approaches, which can lead to greater happiness and success.

Finally, encouragement has the power to improve performance, boost self-esteem, and enhance relationships. Having someone cheering you on will make you feel capable of anything and will motivate you to achieve your best. Furthermore, gaining encouragement from others may increase your morale and help you feel more confident in pursuing your objectives.

Encouragement is a great asset for everyone seeking success. People might be encouraged to pursue their aspirations if they get regular support and direction. Anyone can achieve great things with the correct mindset, a little perseverance, and a little support along the way.

*15 Steps to Achieving Success Through Encouragement

1. Begin each day with a good goal. Visualize your desired outcome and take the time to reconfirm your resolve and commitment.
2. Spend time with folks who motivate and encourage you. Surround yourself with good individuals who can encourage and inspire you.
3. Take frequent breaks throughout the day. Make time for rest and relaxation so that you can remain focused and invigorated.
4. Concentrate on the things that make you happy. Doing things you like may help you stay motivated and productive.
5. Establish attainable objectives. To keep on track and responsible for your performance, set SMART (Specific, Measurable, Achievable, Realistic, Time-bound) objectives.
6. Rejoice at minor victories. Recognizing little victories along the road is essential for staying motivated to achieve greater goals.
7. Seek help from others. When you need assistance, both professionally and personally, ask for it. Nobody can do it alone!
8. Have faith in yourself and the process. Developing self-confidence is essential for success; remember that errors are part of the learning and growing process.
9. Concentrate on solutions rather than issues. When faced with an issue, take a positive attitude and remember to keep focused on how you can overcome it rather than becoming mired down in anxiety or uncertainty.

10. Prioritize self-care. To sustain emotional and mental well-being, prioritize physical exercise, nutrition, relaxation, and other types of self-care.

11. Reward yourself for your efforts and hard work. Treat yourself for accomplishing goals, no matter how large or little, to keep yourself motivated.

12. Recognize and capitalize on your own skills. Knowing what distinguishes you from others might help you achieve in situations where others may not have the same resources or skill set.

13. Keep track of your development and make any adjustments. Track your progress and make modifications as required by tracking your efforts on a regular basis.

14. Plan ahead of time to stay organized. Prioritize work and set deadlines for yourself to stay organized and make progress toward your objectives.

15. Look at the larger picture to stay inspired and motivated. Remember why you started on this journey and keep focused on the larger picture to stay dedicated to your road to success!

*The Transformative Impact of Encouragement(from self doubt to self assurance)

When it comes to attaining achievement, encouragement is a vital tool. It may be utilized to assist someone transform their perspective from one of self-doubt to one of self-assurance. Encouragement provides positive reinforcement and aids in the creation of an environment favorable to development and advancement.

The first step in using encouragement for success is determining which kind of encouragement will be most useful to the person. Everyone reacts differently to encouragement, and knowing the requirements of the person may make all the difference. Some individuals, for example, may benefit from simple words of affirmation, but others may need more concrete types of encouragement, such as prizes for achieving certain objectives.

The next stage is to apply the proper type of encouragement on a regular and consistent basis. This entails offering frequent and insightful feedback as well as acknowledging achievements as they occur. Furthermore, it is critical that the receiver knows why their efforts are being recognized and acknowledged; this helps to establish an awareness that their activities are being seen and respected.

Finally, although encouraging someone to strive for success is essential, it is also crucial to concentrate on the process rather than the end. Achieving success requires hard effort, commitment, and many missteps along the way. As a result, it is critical to acknowledge and reward work in order to promote a growth attitude and prepare the person to tackle any problems that may emerge. Encouragement is a great tool for assisting people in achieving success and reaching their full potential. It is possible to develop confidence and create an atmosphere conducive to growth and advancement by offering positive reinforcement and knowing the individual's specific requirements.

*Using Encouragement to Transform Setbacks into Stepping Stones to Success

The road to success is often filled with challenges and setbacks. This can lead to feelings of frustration, stress, and discouragement. To help combat this, it is important to remember the power of encouragement. Encouragement can help us stay motivated and inspired, even in the face of adversity.

Encouragement can take many forms, but it generally involves providing positive reinforcement and support. This could include cheering someone on, giving compliments, offering helpful advice, or simply lending an ear when someone needs to talk about their struggles. These little acts of kindness can help people recognize that they have the strength and resilience to overcome obstacles. Encouragement also helps to build self-esteem. This is especially true when people receive recognition for their hard work and dedication. Feeling appreciated and valued can give someone the confidence to keep pushing forward and make progress toward their goals.

On the flip side, discouragement can be equally damaging. When people receive criticism and negative feedback, it can make them feel unworthy or inadequate. This can be detrimental to self-confidence and sap their motivation to continue trying. That's why it's so important to choose our words carefully and remember that everyone has their own journey in life.

At the end of the day, success requires a lot of hard work and determination. But it can also be helped along with the encouragement we provide each other. By offering positive reinforcement and constructive feedback, we can help people transform setbacks into stepping stones to success

*How Encouragement Can Help You Overcome Procrastination and Achieve Your goal

We all have goals that we want to reach. However, when it comes to taking action, it is all too simple to put it off. When it comes to attaining our goals and objectives, procrastination may be a huge impediment. The good news is that encouragement may play an important role in assisting us to overcome these hurdles and eventually achieve progress toward the objectives we have set for ourselves.

Encouragement is one of the most effective strategies for keeping us motivated and taking action toward our objectives. It enables us to tap into our inner abilities and resources, as well as overcome any fear or uncertainty that may be preventing us from reaching our objectives.

When we are encouraged by others, we are more likely to perceive our own potential and think that we can achieve our goals. This may help us gain confidence and the strength and bravery to take the essential actions toward our objectives. Encouragement may also help us remain focused and keep going when things become difficult.

It is vital to remember that encouragement may come from oneself as well as from others. Self-encouragement is a really strong tool for overcoming procrastination and taking action on our objectives. We must value ourselves, concentrate on our abilities, and be our own greatest cheerleaders.

Positive self-talk is the most effective type of self-encouragement. When we are feeling demotivated or overwhelmed by the work at hand, positive self-talk may help us re-energize and remain focused on our objectives. We should be careful of the language we use and concentrate on positive affirmations about ourselves and our talents while participating in positive self-talk.

Encouragement is a critical component in achieving any objective. It is important to note that it may originate from both external and internal sources. Anything is achievable with the correct mentality and enough desire! So, while you continue on your path to success, remember to offer yourself some encouragement and remind yourself of your potential.

*Building Confidence Through Encouragement

Encouragement is one of the most effective tools for assisting us in reaching our objectives. It is sometimes said that success starts with believing in oneself. When confronted with challenging responsibilities and self-doubt, it may be difficult to believe in ourselves. That is why words of support from others may mean so much.

Family, friends, and even strangers may provide encouragement. Positive words of praise, admiration and support may boost our confidence and ability. When we are encouraged, we are more inclined to think that we can face a problem and succeed. Even the slightest words of encouragement may have a significant impact on how we see our talents.

Encouragement assists us in overcoming our fears of failure and negative self-talk. It gives us the confidence to take chances and attempt new things, even when we are afraid. And, when we fall short of our objectives, encouragement may help us remain inspired and go on.

Most significantly, encouragement may aid in the development of resilience. According to research, encouraging comments may have a long-term impact on our self-esteem and general mental health. We can confront challenging obstacles and strive for greater achievement if we have a stronger feeling of self-worth. Encouragement is a very effective technique for obtaining achievement. It is important to remember that everyone of us has the ability to improve the lives of others. We may assist people to grow confidence and strive for excellence by delivering gentle words of praise, gratitude, and support. So remember to inspire yourself and the people around you—you never know what a difference you may make.

*Understanding How Encouragement Boosts Success and Happiness

When it comes to achieving success and happiness, we all need some motivation. Friends, family, mentors, and coworkers may all make a significant influence in our lives. It may help us remain motivated when times are rough and drive us closer to our objectives. Encouragement is more than simply praises and praise. It is a kind of positive reinforcement that assists us in being focused and on course. Someone who inspires us and helps us believe in ourselves and our talents. It increases our confidence in our judgments and our resistance to setbacks.

Encouragement also aids in the development of a growth mentality. When we hear encouraging comments, we become more willing to take chances, learn new things, and attempt new tactics. This may help us achieve achievement more quickly and meaningfully. We learn to endure in the face of adversity and to see failure as a chance for growth rather than a sign of defeat.

Encouragement not only increases our chances of achievement, but it also increases our general satisfaction. According to research, persons who are encouraged by others have better levels of self-confidence, happiness, and pleasure. Knowing we have a network of individuals who believe in us may help us form meaningful connections, overcome problems, and live more fulfilled lives. Understanding how encouragement increases achievement and happiness may help us make the most of every opportunity. We may gain confidence in our choices and take strides toward our objectives by seeking support from others around us.

CHAPTER 11

*The Key to Unlocking Your Full Potential and Achieving Your Dreams

We all want to be successful, but sometimes it can feel like an impossible feat. It can be hard to stay motivated, and it's easy to become discouraged when things don't go your way. However, success doesn't have to be out of reach – with the right kind of encouragement, you can unlock your full potential and achieve your dreams.

Encouragement is a powerful tool that can help you stay motivated and inspired. When you receive words of encouragement, you are reminded that you are capable of achieving great things, even if it may seem like an uphill battle. It's important to remember that success comes through hard work, dedication, and self-belief, and that no matter how difficult it may seem, anything is possible with the right attitude.

The best way to encourage yourself is to start by setting achievable goals. Don't set yourself up for failure by aiming too high; instead, break your goal into smaller, more achievable pieces so that you can work your way up to the end result. Celebrate each milestone as you work towards your overall goal and be proud of the progress that you have made.

Find mentors or role models who have achieved similar goals and use their stories as motivation for your own journey. Look for positive examples of success – such as stories about people overcoming obstacles or challenges – and use them as proof that you can do the same. Even when times get tough, remind yourself that anything is possible with a little bit of effort and a lot of determination.

Finally, take time to recognize your own successes. Acknowledge the efforts that you have made and give yourself credit for your hard work. No one else can tell you what success looks like for you, so make sure to take pride in your accomplishments and reward yourself for the progress that you have made.

Remember: with encouragement and dedication, anything is possible. Embrace the power of positive thinking, stay focused on your goals, and never give up on yourself – and soon enough, you'll be able to unlock your full potential and achieve your dreams!

*Harnessing the Benefits of Encouragement for Success

Encouragement is a powerful tool for achieving our objectives and reaching our full potential. It gives us the energy and inspiration we need to keep going and never give up. While there are numerous factors that contribute to success, encouragement is critical in retaining the confidence and desire required to attain your goals.

When we get encouragement, it lifts us up and gives us the strength to persevere even when things are difficult. We become more robust, our self-esteem rises, and our willingness to accept chances rises. It may be quite empowering and encouraging to know that someone has trust in us and believes in us.

Encouragement may also help us keep on track and avoid being sidetracked by setbacks. We are more likely to remain on course when we are surrounded by positive and supporting people. We acquire confidence in our talents and a stronger feeling of self-belief. Furthermore, when we are encouraged, it aids in the development of connections. We feel more linked to individuals who believe in us and on whom we can count for assistance. This allows us to build a strong social network that may assist us to get through tough times and enjoy our accomplishments.

At the end of the day, success is defined by having the bravery to take chances and the confidence to persevere no matter how difficult things seem. Encouragement may provide us with the positive reinforcement and drive we need to keep on track. It is important to remember that if you want to be successful, you must never give up on yourself. Accept the power of encouragement from people who believe in you and utilize it to propel you toward your objectives.

*Transforming Your Mindset through Encouragement

Encouragement is an important part of personal growth and success. When you experience encouragement, it helps you to recognize your strengths and realize what you can achieve. Having someone in your corner cheering you on can do wonders for your motivation, determination, and self-confidence. Encouragement also provides a source of positive energy that can help you make the most out of difficult situations.

When it comes to using encouragement to transform your mindset, there are several key aspects to consider. First, be sure to speak positively to yourself. This means avoiding negative self-talk or speaking out loud about any doubts or fears you have. Instead, look for things that you can feel good about and celebrate your progress. It's also helpful to focus on the process rather than the outcome – when you set achievable goals and follow through, this can help you to build momentum and move forward with confidence.

It's also important to surround yourself with people who support you and believe in your potential. Positive relationships can provide a valuable source of emotional and mental strength, which can be incredibly helpful when times get tough. If you're struggling to find this type of support within your own network, then don't hesitate to seek out resources elsewhere – talking to a counselor or joining a support group are both great options.

Finally, take time to recognize your accomplishments and give yourself credit for each success. Celebrating small victories and recognizing the effort you put into your endeavors is a great way to stay motivated and remember why you're striving towards a specific goal.

The power of encouragement is undeniable – by focusing on positive self-talk and actively seeking out supportive relationships, you can start to transform your mindset in order to achieve success.

Remember, never give up on yourself – no matter how tough things may seem

*The Connection Between Encouragement and Goal-Setting

Goal achievement requires a high level of motivation. When it comes to achieving your objectives, having someone in your corner who supports you and keeps you on track may make all the difference. It comes as no surprise that there is a link between encouragement and goal-setting.

The activity of providing someone support, confidence, or hope is characterized as encouragement. Having the courage and desire to keep going even when things become rough is a key component of developing and attaining objectives. Encouragement from loved ones may assist individuals in remaining motivated and achieving their objectives.

Encouragement may take many different forms. When circumstances are bad, it may be a nice remark, praise, or a pat on the back. It may also take the form of something more practical, such as giving assistance with a project or advice on how to handle a situation. Encouragement, in whatever form, is a powerful tool that may help individuals achieve their objectives.

Encouragement not only keeps us motivated to keep going, but it also gives us confidence that we can achieve our objectives. When someone believes in us and expresses confidence in our capacity to achieve our objectives, it gives us an additional push of confidence and resolve.

Goal-setting and encouragement go hand in hand. It is important to have someone in your corner to give support and encouragement while you work toward your objectives. Encouragement gives us the desire and confidence to keep going even when things seem unattainable. So, the next time you're feeling down, remember to seek some encouragement from someone who believes in you. Anything is achievable with the correct amount of support and drive!

*The Positive Impact of Encouragement on Personal Relationships and Communication

Encouragement is a vital feature of personal relationships and communication. It has a profound influence on others around us, allowing us to connect in meaningful ways, create trust, and form deep ties.

We validate others' thoughts and experiences when we support them, making them feel appreciated and understood. We demonstrate that we are concerned about their well-being, which encourages them to open up and share more with us. It also aids in the development of self-esteem and confidence, helping individuals to trust themselves and form stronger relationships.

Encouragement also improves two-person communication. It enables us to better comprehend each other's points of view and demonstrates that we appreciate what the other person has to say. When we are encouraged, we become more inclined to listen and offer our whole attention, which promotes better dialogues. This open communication also helps us to communicate our demands in a healthy manner, which strengthens our bond with one another.

Aside from these practical advantages, encouragement contributes to the creation of a pleasant atmosphere that improves emotions of safety and security. Knowing that our emotions are recognized and respected by others gives us the confidence to take chances and develop as people. We can trust that if things don't go as planned, we will be supported, which may lead to increased self-confidence and resilience.

Overall, the importance of encouragement cannot be overstated. It may have a significant impact on our personal relationships and communication, resulting in stronger bonds, better understanding, and higher self-esteem. So, the next time you connect with someone, consider how you might encourage them and make a difference in their lives.

*The Benefits of Encouragement for Athletes

Athletes of all levels, from newbie to professional, have long recognized the value of encouragement in attaining success. Encouragement may come from a variety of sources, including teammates, coaches, and family members. It is a formidable weapon with the capacity to boost confidence, develop motivation and devotion, and assist athletes in overcoming challenges.

The importance of encouragement in attaining achievement cannot be overstated. A Stanford University research found that when students received positive comments and peer support, their motivation, grades, and performance increased dramatically. Athletes who are encouraged to believe in themselves, establish goals, and strive for perfection are more likely to succeed than those who are not supported.

Encouragement also aids athletes in remaining focused on the job at hand. Athletes who are frustrated or stressed may lose concentration and become easily sidetracked. Positive reinforcement, on the other hand, may provide a much-needed lift, helping athletes to stay on course despite adversity.

Finally, encouraging athletes might help them create a growth attitude. According to research, athletes who are commended for their efforts rather than their ability tend to be more successful in the long run. Athletes with a growth mindset recognize that they can enhance their talents via hard effort and devotion. This motivates individuals to continue striving for greatness in the face of hardship.

In conclusion, the advantages of encouraging athletes are broad and far-reaching. Athletes may achieve success in any sector if they have the correct mindset and support from the people around them. Athletes may unleash a new level of drive and confidence that will push them to greatness by concentrating on their efforts rather than outcomes and believing in themselves and their skills.

*<u>Encouragement and the Journey to Self-Acceptance</u>

We all have the capacity for greatness and achievement, but the road to get there may be challenging. Self-doubt and fear may often get in the way of our goals, making it difficult to remain focused and motivated. That is why it is important to seek out sources of support along the route.

Encouragement is a strong instrument that may give us the boost we need to keep going and accomplish our objectives. It may take various forms, from friends and family providing words of encouragement and comfort to mentors and role models demonstrating how to realize our full potential.

We must keep in mind that encouragement is more than simply words; it is also an act of comprehension and acceptance. When someone encourages us, they see that we have the capacity for greatness, even if we don't believe in ourselves.

Encouragement does not necessarily need to come from outside sources; it may also come from inside. Self-encouragement is a strong weapon that we may use to raise ourselves up and keep going when things become difficult. Taking the time to recognize your own successes, enjoy your wins, and recognize your qualities is what self-encouragement entails.

Encouragement may be a helpful tool for development and achievement on the path to self-acceptance. We may establish a road to achievement and real self-fulfillment by embracing our potential and allowing ourselves permission to dream large.

CONCLUSION

This book is based on my need to learn to use encouragement as a tool to help you to develop your thoughts about what and how encouragement can be used as fuel to your success. You cannot amend, distribute, sell, use, quote or paraphrase any part, or the content within this book, without consent of the author or publisher. Success Through Encouragement is more than a catchphrase; it is a way of life. It is all about establishing a good and supportive atmosphere in which people may grow and attain their greatest potential. Consider a world where all members of your team are encouraged to take chances, try new things, and learn from their failures without fear of failure. Encouragement is a powerful tool for achieving success. It serves as the catalyst for growth and development. A supportive environment is essential to success. Never let our environment, people, or circumstances determine if we can succeed. It is our confidence, belief, and having faith in ourselves that will empower us to rise above any adversity and achieve greatness. Encouragement in the workplace can enhance employee motivation and engagement by adding flavor, depth, and richness to the workplace culture. It has the potential to foster a good and supportive work atmosphere in which people feel heard, understood, and valued. It can also aid in the retention of top talent since employees who feel valued and appreciated are more inclined to stay with the organization. Having a positive attitude is one of the most important factors in an employee's success. Individuals need encouragement from their leaders, and employees are empowered by positive reinforcement. Employee engagement is a three-part cycle that begins with intrinsic drive. This can be accomplished through encouragement or the development of connections that foster positive behaviour and attitudes. Encouragement is a critical component of success and is required for goal setting, achievement, and maintenance. According to research, encouragement can improve performance, self-concept, and competence, and good feedback is related with tenacity when confronted with difficult conditions. Encouragement does not always imply being too enthusiastic or cheerleading others; it should be a particular action taken in support of someone else's efforts. Positive feedback is a great instrument for achieving achievement. When individuals on a team feel encouraged, they are more likely to work together towards a common goal. This kind of open communication and collaboration increases trust and allows for better understanding among team members. It also encourages risk taking and creative thinking, which can lead to innovative solutions to complex problems. Effective communication is an essential part of developing relationships, setting and meeting expectations, motivating, and recognizing achievement. It can be a powerful tool for motivating someone to reach their goals and instilling in them a belief that hard work and effort will result in positive outcomes. By recognizing successes, and celebrating accomplishments, a person can gain self-confidence and understand that their efforts to pay off. Encouragement is associated with greater emotional regulation, reduced anxiety and a decrease in depression and burnout. When people feel encouraged, they tend to take risks and take chances they wouldn't have taken otherwise. This allows individuals to find creative solutions to their problems, further reducing stress and enhancing well-being. Mentorship and coaching can be extremely beneficial when trying to encourage success in others. Encouragement is a key factor in stimulating creativity and fostering an environment that encourages creative growth and exploration. Research has found that encouragement of creative pursuits leads to improved creativity outcomes and a more positive attitude toward creative activities. When a person is encouraged, they can be more motivated and inspired to think of new and innovative ideas. Encouragement plays a vital role in fostering a culture of innovation by boosting morale, creating a supportive environment, promoting risk-taking, increasing motivation, fostering collaboration, and supporting experimentation. A positive work environment, where employees feel encouraged and supported, can lead to increased job satisfaction and reduced likelihood of turnover. Encouragement can also have a significant impact on employee retention and loyalty. Recognition and rewards can have a positive impact on employee retention and loyalty by improving job satisfaction, increasing motivation, fostering a positive work environment, enhancing relationships, boosting confidence, and recognizing achievements. Allowing employees to have a healthy work-life balance can increase motivation and drive, as they feel more energized and fulfilled in both their personal and professional lives. Encouraging a balance between work and personal life is crucial for overall well-being and success. Encouragement can have a significant impact on overall organizational success by improving employee morale, boosting motivation and productivity, enhancing collaboration, fostering innovation, attracting top talent, and supporting a positive workplace culture. In conclusion, encouraging a balance between work and personal life is important for overall well-being, reducing stress, enhancing relationships, increasing motivation, supporting work-life integration, and to attract top talent. Encouragement plays a vital role in overcoming obstacles and challenges by boosting confidence, building resilience, increasing motivation, providing support, recognizing achievements, and fostering growth and learning. Encouraging success through building resilience and perseverance can lead to improved outcomes and overall success. It can help individuals develop problem-solving skills, foster a growth mindset, increase motivation, and foster continuous learning and improvement. People with higher emotional intelligence are better able to receive and give positive reinforcement, and provide encouragement in order to boost their own and others' morale. Encouragement is a crucial tool for managing stress, achieving goals, and having meaningful relationships with others. It can have a positive impact on personal and professional development by boosting confidence, supporting continuous learning and increasing motivation.